INTERNATIONAL LANGUAGE

INTERNATIONAL LANGUAGE

PAST, PRESENT & FUTURE

WITH SPECIMENS OF ESPERANTO
AND GRAMMAR

BY W. J. CLARK

M.A. OXON., PH.D. LEIPZIG

LICENCIÉ-ÈS-LETTRES, BACHELIER-EN-DROIT
PARIS

LONDON
J. M. DENT & COMPANY
1907

PRINTED BY
HAZELL, WATSON AND VINEY, LD.,
LONDON AND AYLESBURY.

PREFACE

An artificial language may be more regular, more perfect, and easier to learn than a natural one.—MAX MÜLLER.

THE world is spinning fast down the grooves of change. The old disorder changeth. Haply it is yielding place to new. The tongue is a little member. It should no longer be allowed to divide the nations.

Two things stand out in the swift change. Science with all its works is spreading to all lands. The East, led by Japan, is coming into line with the West.

Standardization of life may fittingly be accompanied by standardization of language. The effect may be twofold— Practical and Ideal.

Practical. The World has a thousand tongues,
            Science but one :
         They'll climb up a thousand rungs
           When Babel's done.

Ideal. Mankind has a thousand tongues,
            Friendship but one :
        Banzai ! then from heart and lungs
          For the Rising Sun.

W. J. C.

NOTE.—The following pages have had the advantage of being read in MS. by Mr. H. Bolingbroke Mudie, and I am indebted to him for many corrections and suggestions.

AN INTERNATIONAL AUXILIARY LANGUAGE

NOTE.—To avoid repeating the cumbrous phrase "international auxiliary language," the word *auxiliary* is usually omitted. It must be clearly understood that when "international" or "universal" language is spoken of, *auxiliary* is also implied.

PART I
GENERAL

CONTENTS

PART II

HISTORICAL

PART III

THE CLAIMS OF ESPERANTO TO BE TAKEN SERIOUSLY:
CONSIDERATIONS BASED ON THE STRUCTURE OF
THE LANGUAGE ITSELF

PART IV

SPECIMENS OF ESPERANTO, WITH GRAMMAR AND
VOCABULARY

CONTENTS

APPENDIX A

APPENDIX B

APPENDIX C

CONTENTS

PART I

GENERAL

I

INTRODUCTORY

In dealing with the problem of the introduction of an international language, we are met on the threshold by two main questions :

1. The question of principle.
2. The question of practice.

By the question of principle is meant, Is it desirable to have a universal language ? do we wish for one ? in short, is there a demand ?

The question of practice includes the inquiries, Is such a language possible ? is it easy ? would its introduction be fraught with prohibitive difficulties ? and the like.

It is clear that, however possible or easy it may be to do a thing, there is no case for doing it unless it is wanted ; therefore the question of principle must be taken first. In the case before us the question of principle involves many considerations— aesthetic, political, social, even religious. These will be glanced at in their proper place ; but for our present purpose they are all subordinate to the one great paramount consideration—the economic one. In the world of affairs experience shows that, given a demand of any kind whatever, as between an economical method of supplying that demand and a non-economical method, in the long run the economical method will surely prevail.

If, then, it can be shown that there is a growing need for means of international communication, and that a unilingual solution is more economical than a multilingual one, there is good ground for thinking that the unilingual method of transacting international affairs will surely prevail. It then becomes a question of time and method : When will men feel the pressure of the demand sufficiently strongly to set about supplying it ? and what means will they adopt?

The time and the method are by no means indifferent. Though a demand (for what is possible) is sure, in the long run, to get itself supplied, a long period of wasteful and needless groping may be avoided by a clear-sighted and timely realization of the demand, and by consequent organized co-operation in supplying it. Intelligent anticipation sometimes helps events to occur. It is the object of this book to call attention to the present state of affairs, and to emphasize the fact that the time is now ripe for dealing with the question, and the present moment propitious for solving the problem once for all in an orderly way. The merest glance at the list of projects for a universal language * and their dates will strengthen the conviction from an historical point of view that the fulness of time is accomplished, while the history of the rise and fall of *Volapük* and of the extraordinary rise of *Esperanto*, in spite of its precursor's failure, are exceedingly significant.

One language has been born, come to maturity, and died of dissension, and the world stood by indifferent. Another is now in the first full flush of youth and strength. After twenty-nine years of daily developing cosmopolitanism—years that have witnessed the rising of a new star in the East and an uninterrupted growth of interchange of ideas between the nations of the earth, whether in politics, literature, or science, without a single check to the ever-rising tide of internationalism—are we again to let the favourable moment pass unused, just for want of making up our minds ? At present one language holds the field. It is well

* See pp. 78–87.

organized ; it has abundant enthusiastic partisans accustomed to communicate and transact their common business in it, and only too anxious to show the way to others. If it be not officially adopted and put under the regulation of a duly constituted international authority, it may wither away or split into factions as Volapük did.* Or it may continue to grow and flourish, but others of its numerous rivals may secure adherents and dispute its claim. This would be even worse. It is far harder to rally a multitude of conflicting rivals in the same camp, than it is to take over a well-organized, homogeneous, and efficient volunteer force, legalize its position, and raise it to the status of a regular army. In any case, if no concerted action be taken, the question will remain in a state of chaos, and the lack of official organization brings a great risk of overlapping, dissension, and creation of rival interests, and generally produces a state of affairs calculated to postpone indefinitely the supply of the demand. Competition that neither tends to keep down the price nor to improve the quality of the thing produced is mere dissipation of energy.

In a word, the one thing needful at present is not a more highly perfected language to adopt, but the adoption of the highly perfected one we possess. By the admission of experts, no less than by the practical experience of great numbers of persons in using it over a number of years, it has been found adequate. Once found adequate, its absolute utility merely depends upon universal adoption.

With utility in direct proportion to numbers of adherents, every recruit augments its value—a thought which may well encourage waverers to make the slight effort necessary to at any rate learn to read it.

---

* Esperanto itself is admirably organized (see p. 119), and there are no factions or symptoms of dissension. But Esperantists need official support and recognition.

II

As stated above, the question of principle will be treated here from a purely economical point of view, since practical value, measured by saving of time, money, and effort, must be the ultimate criterion by which the success or failure of so far-reaching a reform as the introduction of an international, auxiliary language will be decided. The bearing of such a reform upon education, culture, race supremacy, etc., is not without importance ; but the discussion of these points must be postponed as subsidiary.

Reduced to its simplest form, the economical argument is this :

(1) The volume of international intercourse is great and increasing.

(2) This intercourse is at present carried on in many different languages of varying degrees of difficulty, but all relatively hard of acquisition for those who do not know them as a mother-tongue. This is uneconomical.

(3) It is economically sounder to carry on international intercourse in one easy language than in a large number of hard ones.

(4) Therefore in principle an easy international language is desirable.

Let us glance at these four points a little more in detail.

No. 1 surely needs no demonstration. Every year there is more communication between men of different race and language. And it is not business, in the narrow sense of the term, that is exclusively or even chiefly affected by diversity of language. Besides the enormous bulk of pleasure travel, international congresses are growing in number and importance ; municipal fraternization is the latest fashion, and many a worthy alderman, touring at the ratepayers' expense, must wish that he had some German in Berlin, or a little Italian in Milan. Indeed, it is at these points of international contact that language is a real bar, actually preventing much intercourse that would otherwise have taken place, rather than in business, which is organized in view of the difficulty. Then there is the whole realm of scientific and learned literature—work of which the accessibility to all concerned is of the first importance, but is often hindered because a translation into one language does not pay, or, if made, only reaches a limited public. Such bars to freedom of interchange cannot be reckoned in money; but modern economics recognizes the personal and social factor, and any obstacle to research is certainly a public loss.

But important as are these various spheres of action, an even wider international contact of thought and feeling is springing up in our days. Democracy, science, and universal education are producing everywhere similarity of institutions, of industry, of the whole organization of life. Similarity of life will breed community of interests, and from this arises real converse—more give and take in the things that matter, less purely superficial dealings of the guide-book or conversation-manual type.

(2) "Business," meaning commerce, in so far as it is inter-national, may at present be carried on mainly in half a dozen of the principal languages of Western Europe. Even so, their multiplicity is vexatious. But outside the world of business other languages are entering the field, and striving for equal rights. The tendency is all towards self-assertion on the part of the nationalities that are beginning a new era of national life and importance. The language difficulty in the Austrian Empire reflects the growing self-consciousness of the Magyars. Everywhere where young peoples are pushing their rights to take equal rank among the nations of the world, the language question is put in the forefront. The politicians of Ireland and Wales have realized the importance of language in asserting nationality, but such engineered language-agitation offers but

a feeble reflex of the vitality of the question in lands where the native language is as much in use for all purposes as is English in England. These lands will fight harder and harder against the claims to supremacy of a handful of Western intruders. A famous foreign philologist,* in a report on the subject presented to the Academy of Vienna, notes the increasing tendency of Russian to take rank among the recognized languages for purposes of polite learning. He is well placed to observe. With Russia knocking at the door and Hungary waiting to storm the breach, what tongue may not our descendants of the next century have to learn, under pain of losing touch with important currents of thought? It is high time something were done to standardize means of transmission. Owing to political conditions, there are linguistically disintegrating forces at work, which are at variance with the integrating forces of natural tendency.

From an economical point of view, a considerable amount of time, effort, and money must be unreproductively invested in overcoming the "language difficulty." In money alone the amount must run into thousands of pounds yearly. Among the unreproductive investments are—the employment of foreign correspondence clerks, the time and money spent upon the installation of educational plant for their production, the time and money spent upon translations and interpreters for the proceedings of international conferences and negotiations, the time devoted by professors and other researchers (often non-linguists in virtue of their calling) to deciphering special treatises and learned periodicals in languages not their own.†

* Prof. Shuchardt.

† These are some of the actual visible losses owing to the *presence* of the language difficulty. No one can estimate the value of the losses entailed by the *absence* of free intercourse due to removable linguistic barriers. Potential (but at present non-realized) extension of goodwill, swifter progress, and wider knowledge represent one side of their value; while consequent non-realized increase in volume of actual business represents their value in money. The negative statement of absence of results from intercourse that never took place affords no measure of positive results obtainable under a better system.

The tendency of those engaged in advancing material progress, which consists in the subjection of nature to man's ends, is to adapt more and more quickly their methods to changing conditions. Has the world yet faced in a business-like spirit the problem of wiping out wastage on words?

Big industrial concerns scrap machinery while it is yet perfectly capable of running and turning out good work, in order to replace it by newer machinery, capable of turning out more work in the same time. Time is money. Can the busy world afford a language difficulty?

(3) The proposition that it is economically sounder to carry on international intercourse in one easy language than in a large number of hard ones rests upon the principle that it does not pay to do a thing a hard way, if the same results can be produced by an easy way.

The whole industrial revolution brought about by the invention of machinery depended upon this principle. Since an artificial language, like machinery, is a means invented by man of furthering his ends, there seems to be no abuse of analogy in comparing them.

When it was found that machinery would turn out a hundred pieces of cloth while the hand-loom turned out one, the hand-loom was doomed, except in so far as it may serve other ends, antiquarian, aesthetic, or artistic, which are not equally well served by machinery. Similarly, to take another revolution which is going on in our own day through a further application of machinery, when it is found that corn can be reaped and threshed by machinery, that hay can be cut, made, carried, and stacked by machinery, that man can travel the high road by machinery, sooner or later machinery is bound to get the bulk of the job, because it produces the same results at greater speed and less cost. So, in the field of international intercourse, if an easy artificial language can with equal efficiency and at less cost produce the same results as a multiplicity of natural ones, in many lines of human activity, and making all reserves in matters antiquarian, aesthetic, and artistic, sooner or later the multiplicity will have to go to the scrap-heap * as cumbrous and out of date.   It may be a hundred years ; it may be fifty ; it may be even twenty.   Almost certainly the irresistible trend of economic pressure will work its will and insist that what has to be done shall be done in the most economical way.

So much, then, for the question of principle.   In treating it, certain large assumptions have been made ; e.g. it is said above, " if an easy artificial language can with equal efficiency . . . produce the same results," etc.   Here it is assumed that the artificial language is (1) easy, and (2) that it is possible for it to produce the same results.   Again, however easy and possible, its introduction might cost more than it saved.   These are questions of fact, and are treated in the three following chapters under the heading of " The Question of Practice."

III

THE QUESTION OF PRACTICE—AN INTERNATIONAL LANGUAGE IS POSSIBLE

THE man who says a thing is impossible without troubling to find out whether it has been done is merely "talking through his hat," to use an Americanism, and we need not waste much time on him.   Any one, who maintains that it is impossible to transact the ordinary business of life and write lucid treatises on scientific and other subjects in an artificial language, is simply in the position of the French engineer, who gave a full scientific demonstration of the fact that an engine could not possibly travel by steam.

The plain fact is that not only one artificial language, but

---

* But only, of course, in those lines in which an international auxiliary language can produce equally good results.   This excludes home use, national literature, philology, scholarly study of national languages, etc.

several, already exist, which not only can express, but already have expressed all the ideas current in social intercourse, business, and serious exposition. It is only necessary to state the facts briefly.

First—*Volapük.*

Three congresses were held in all for the promotion of this language. The third (Paris, 1889) was the most important. It was attended by Volapükists from many different nations, who carried on all their business in Volapük, and found no difficulty in understanding one another. Besides this, there were a great many newspapers published in Volapük, which treated of all kinds of subjects.

Secondly—*Idiom Neutral*, the lineal descendant of Volapük.

It is regulated by an international academy, which sends round circulars and does all its business in Idiom Neutral.

Thirdly—*Esperanto.*

Since the publication of the language in 1887 it has had a gradually increasing number of adherents, who have used it for all ordinary purposes of communication. A great number of newspapers and reviews of all kinds are now published regularly in Esperanto in a great variety of countries. I take up a chance number of the *Internacia Scienca Revuo*, which happens to be on my table, and find the following subjects among the contents of the month : " *Rôle* of living beings in the general physiology of the earth," " The carnivorous animals of Sweden," " The part played by heredity in the etiology of chronic nephritis," " The migration of the lemings," " Notices of books," " Notes and correspondence," etc. In fact, the Review has all the appearance of an ordinary scientific periodical, and the articles are as clearly expressed and as easy to read as those in any similar review in a national language.

Even more convincing perhaps, for the uninitiated, is the evidence afforded by the International Congresses of Esperantists. The first was held at Boulogne in August 1905. It marked an epoch in the lives of many of the participants, whose doubts as to the practical nature of an artificial language there, for good and all, yielded to the logic of facts ; and it may well be that it will some day be rather an outstanding landmark in the history of civilization. A brief description will, therefore, not be out of place.

In the little seaport town on the north coast of France had come together men and women of more than twenty different races. Some were experts, some were beginners ; but all save a very few must have been alike in this, that they had learnt their Esperanto at home, and, as far as oral use went, had only been able to speak it (if at all) with members of their own national groups—that is, with compatriots who had acquired the language under the same conditions as to pronunciation, etc., as themselves. Experts and beginners, those who from practical experience knew the great possibilities of the new tongue as a written medium, no less than the neophytes and tentative experimenters who had come to see whether the thing was worth taking seriously, they were now to make the decisive trial—in the one case to test the faith that was in them, in the other to set all doubt at rest in one sense or the other for good and all.

The town theatre had been generously placed at the disposal of the Congress, and the author of the language, Dr. Zamenhof, had left his eye-patients at Warsaw and come to preside at the coming out of his *kara lingvo*, now well on in her 'teens, and about to leave the academic seclusion of scholastic use and emerge into the larger sphere of social and practical activity.

On Saturday evening, August 5, at eight o'clock, the Boulogne Theatre was packed with a cosmopolitan audience. The unique assembly was pervaded by an indefinable feeling of expectancy ; as in the lull before the thunderstorm, there was the hush of excitement, the tense silence charged with the premonition of some vast force about to be let loose on the world. After a few preliminaries, there was a really dramatic moment when Dr. Zamenhof stood up for the first time to address his world-audience in the world-tongue. Would they understand him ?

Was their hope about to be justified? or was it all a chimera, "such stuff as dreams are made on"?

"*Gesinjoroj*" (= Ladies and gentlemen)—the great audience craned forward like one man, straining eyes and ears towards the speaker,—"*Kun granda plezuro mi akceptis la proponon . . .*" The crowd drank in the words with an almost pathetic agony of anxiety. Gradually, as the clear-cut sentences poured forth in a continuous stream of perfect lucidity, and the audience realized that they were all listening to and all understanding a really international speech in a really international tongue—a tongue which secured to them, as here in Boulogne so throughout the world, full comprehension and a sense of comradeship and fellow-citizenship on equal terms with all users of it—the anxiety gave way to a scene of wild enthusiasm. Men shook hands with perfect strangers, and all cheered and cheered again. Zamenhof finished with a solemn declamation of one of his hymns (given as an appendix to this volume, with translation), embodying the lofty ideal which has inspired him all through and sustained him through the many difficulties he has had to face. When he came to the end, the fine passage beginning with the words, "*Ni inter popoloj la murojn detruos*" ("we shall throw down the walls between the peoples"), and ending "*amo kaj vero ekregos sur tero*" ("love and truth shall begin their reign on earth"), the whole concourse rose to their feet with prolonged cries of "Vivu Zamenhof!"

No doubt this enthusiasm may sound rather forced and unreal to those who have not attended a congress, and the cheers may ring hollow across intervening time and space. Neither would it be good for this or any movement to rely upon facile enthusiasm, as easily damped as aroused. There is something far more than this in the international language movement.

At the same time, it is impossible for any one who has not tried it to realize the thrill—not a weak, sentimental thrill, but a reasonable thrill, starting from objective fact and running down the marrow of things—given by the first real contact with an international language in an international setting. There really is a feeling as of a new power born into the world.

Those who were present at the Geneva Congress, 1906, will not soon forget the singing of the song "La Espero" at the solemn closing of the week's proceedings. The organ rolled out the melody, and when the gathered thousands that thronged the floor of the hall and packed the galleries tier on tier to the ceiling took up the opening phrase—

> En la mondon venis nova sento,
> Tra la mondo iras forta voko,*

they meant every word of it. It was a fitting summary of the impressions left by the events of the week, and what the lips uttered must have been in the hearts and minds of all.

As an ounce of personal experience is worth a pound of second-hand recital, a brief statement may here be given of the way in which the present writer came to take up Esperanto, and of the experiences which soon led him to the conviction of its absolute practicability and utility.

In October, 1905, having just returned from an absence of some years in Canada and the Far East, he had his attention turned to Esperanto for the first time by reading an account of the Congress of Boulogne. He had no previous knowledge of, or leanings towards, a universal language; and if he had thought about it at all, it was only to laugh at the idea as a wild and visionary scheme. In short, his attitude was quite normal.

But here was a definite statement, professing to be one of positive accomplished fact. One of two things : either the newspaper account was not true; or else, the facts being as represented, here was a new possibility to be reckoned with. The only course was to send for the books and test the thing on its merits. Being somewhat used to languages, he did not take long to see that this one was good enough in itself. A letter, written in

---

* Into the world has come a new feeling,
  Through the world goes a mighty call.

Esperanto, after a few days' study of the grammar at odd times, with a halfpenny Esperanto-English key enclosed, was fully understood by the addressee, though he was ignorant up till then of the very existence of Esperanto. This experience has often been since repeated ; indeed, the correspondent will often write back after a few days in Esperanto. Such letters have always been found intelligible, though in no case did the correspondent know Esperanto previously. The experiment is instructive and amusing, and can be tried by any one for an expenditure of twopence for keys and a few hours for studying the sixteen rules and their application. To many minds these are far simpler and more easy to grasp for practical use than the rules for scoring at bridge.

After a month or two's playing with the language in spare time, the writer further tested it, by sending out a flight of postcards to various selected Esperantists' addresses in different parts of the Russian Empire. The addressees ranged from St. Petersburg and Helsingfors through Poland to the Caucasus and to far Siberia. In nearly every case answers were received, and in some instances the initial interchange of postcards led to an extremely interesting correspondence, throwing much light on the disturbed state of things in the native town or province of the correspondent. From a Tiflis doctor came a graphic account of the state of affairs in the Caucasus ; while a school inspector from the depths of Eastern Siberia painted a vivid picture of the effect of political unrest on the schools—lockouts and "malodorous chemical obstructions" (*Anglice*—the schools were stunk out). Many writers expressed themselves with great freedom, but feared their letters would not pass the censor. Judging by the proportion of answers received, the censorship was not at that time efficient. In no case was there any difficulty in grasping the writer's meaning. All the answers were in Esperanto.

This was fairly convincing, but still having doubts on the question of pronunciation, the writer resolved to attend the Esperanto Congress to be held at Geneva in August 1906. To this end he continued to read Esperanto at odd minutes and took in an Esperanto gazette. About three weeks before the congress he got a member of his family to read aloud to him every day as far as possible a page or two of Esperanto, in order to attune his ear. He never had an opportunity of speaking the language before the congress, except once for a few minutes, when he travelled some distance to attend a meeting of the nearest English group.

Thus equipped, he went through the Congress of Geneva, and found himself able to follow most of the proceedings, and to converse freely, though slowly, with people of the most diverse nationality. At an early sitting of the congress he found himself next to a Russian from Kischineff, who had been through the first great *pogrom*, and a most interesting conversation ensued. Another day the neighbours were an Indian nawab and an abbé from Madrid. Another time it was a Bulgarian. At the first official banquet he sat next to a Finn, who rejoiced in the name of Attila, and, but for the civilizing influence of a universal language, might have been in the sunny south, like his namesake of the ancient world, on a very different errand from his present peaceful one. Yet here he was, rubbing elbows with Italians, as if there had never been such things as Huns or a sack of Rome by northern barbarians.

During the meal a Frenchman, finding himself near us English and some Germans, proposed a toast to the "entente cordiale taking in Germany," which was honoured with great enthusiasm. This is merely an instance of the small ways in which such gatherings make for peace and good will.

With all these people it was perfectly easy to converse in the common tongue, pronunciation and national idiom being no bar in practice.

And this experience was general throughout the duration of the congress. Day by day sittings were held for the transaction of all kinds of business and the discussion of the most varied subjects. It was impressive to see people from half the countries of the world rise from different corners of the hall and contribute their share to the discussion in the most matter-of-fact way. Day by day the congressists met in social functions, debates, lectures, and sectional groups (chemical, medical, legal, etc.) for the regulation of matters touching their special interests. Everything was done in Esperanto, and never was there the slightest hitch or misunderstanding, or failure to give adequate expression to opinions owing to defects of language. The language difficulty was annihilated.

Perhaps one of the most striking demonstrations of this return to pre-Babel conditions was the performance of a three-part comedy by a Frenchman, a Russian, and a Spaniard. Such a thing would inevitably have been grotesque in any national language; but here they met on common neutral ground. No one's accent was "foreign," and none of the spectators possessed that mother-tongue acquaintance with Esperanto that would lead them to feel slight divergences shocking, or even noticeable without extreme attention to the point. Other theatrical performances were given at Geneva, as also at Boulogne, where a play of Molière was performed in Esperanto by actors of eight nationalities with one rehearsal, and with full success.

In the face of these facts it is idle to oppose a universal artificial language on the score of impossibility or inadequacy. The theoretical pronunciation difficulty completely crumbled away before the test of practice.

The "war-at-any-price party," the whole-hoggers *à tous crins* (the juxtaposition of the two national idioms lends a certain realism, and heightens the effect of each), are therefore driven back on their second line of attack, if the Hibernianism may be excused. "Yes," they say, "your language may be possible, but, after all, why not learn an existing language, if you've got to learn one anyway?"

Now, quite apart from the obvious fact that the nations will never agree to give the preference to the language of one of them to the prejudice of the others, this argument involves the

suggestion that an artificial language is no easier to learn
than a natural one. We thus come to the question of ease as a
qualification.

IV

THE QUESTION OF PRACTICE (*continued*)—AN INTERNATIONAL LANGUAGE IS EASY *

PEOPLE smile incredulously at the mention of an artificial
language, implying that no easy royal road can be found to
language-learning of any kind. But the odds are all the other
way, and they are heavy odds.

The reason for this is quite simple, and may be briefly put
as follows :

The object of language is to express thought and feeling.
Every natural language contains all kinds of complications and
irregularities, which are of no use whatever in attaining this
object, but merely exist because they happen to have grown.
Their sole *raison d'être* is historical. In fact, for a language
without a history they are *unnecessary.*† Therefore a universal
language, whose only object is to supply to every one the
simplest possible means of expressing his thoughts and feelings
in a medium intelligible to every one else, simply leaves them
out. Now, it is precisely in these " unnecessary " complications
that a large proportion—certainly more than half—of the
difficulty of learning a foreign language consists. Therefore an
artificial language, by merely leaving them out, becomes
certainly more than twice as easy to learn as any natural
language.

* Readers who do not care about the reasons for this, but desire concrete
proofs, may skip the next few pages and turn in to p. 20, par. 6.

† i.e. they do not assist in attaining its object as a language. One universal
way of forming the plural, past tense, or comparative expresses plurality,
past time, or comparison just as well as fifteen ways, and with a deal less
trouble.

A little reflection will make this truth so absurdly obvious, that the only wonder is, not that it is now beginning to be recognized, but that any one could have ever derided it.

That the "unnecessary" difficulties of a natural language are more than one-half of the whole is certainly an under-estimate; for some languages the proportion would be more like 3 : 4 or 5 : 6. Compared with these, the artificial language would be three times to five times as easy.

Take an illustration. Compare the work to be done by the learner of (a) Latin, (b) Esperanto, in expressing past, present, and future action.

(a) Latin:

Present tense active is expressed by—

> 6 endings in the 1st regular conjugation.
> 6   "   2nd   "
> 6   "   3rd   "
> 6   "   4th   "

Total regular endings : 24.

To these must be added a vast number of quite different and varying forms for irregular verbs.

(b) Esperanto :

Present tense active is expressed by—

> 1 ending for every verb in the language.

Total regular and irregular endings : 1.

It is exactly the same for the past and future.

Total endings for the 3 tenses active :

(a) Latin : 72 regular forms, plus a very large number of irregular and defective verbs.

(b) Esperanto : 3 forms.

Turning to the passive voice, we get—

(a) Latin : A complete set of different endings, some of them puzzling in form and liable to confusion with other parts of the verb.

2

(*b*) Esperanto : No new endings at all.   Merely the three-form regular active conjugation of the verb *esti* = to be, with a passive participle.   No confusion possible.

It is just the same with compound tenses, subjunctives, participles, etc.   Making all due allowances, it is quite safe to say that the Latin verb is fifty times as hard as the Esperanto verb.

The proportion would be about the same in the case of substantives, Latin having innumerable types.

Comparing modern languages with Esperanto, the proportion in favour of the latter would not be so high as fifty to one in the inflection of verbs and nouns, though even here it would be very great, allowing for subjunctives, auxiliaries, irregularities, etc.   But taking the whole languages, it might well rise to ten to one.

For what are the chief difficulties in language-learning ?

They are mainly either difficulties of phonetics, or of structure and vocabulary.

Difficulties of phonetics are :

(1) Multiplicity of sounds to be produced, including many sounds and combinations that do not occur in the language of the learner.

(2) Variation of accent, and of sounds expressed by the same letter.

These difficulties are both eliminated in Esperanto.

(1) Relatively few sounds are adopted into the language, and only such as are common to nearly all languages.   For instance, there are only five full vowels and three * diphthongs, which can be explained to every speaker in terms of his own language.   All the modified vowels, closed " u's " and "e's," half tones, longs and shorts, open and closed vowels, etc., which form the chief bugbear in correct pronunciation, and often render the foreigner unintelligible—all these disappear.

(2) There is no variation of accent or of sound expressed by

* Omitting the rare *eŭ*.   *ej* and *uj* are merely simple vowels plus consonantal *j* (= English *y*).

the same letter. The principle "one letter, one sound"* is adhered to absolutely. Thus, having learned one simple rule for accent (always on the last syllable but one), and the uniform sound corresponding to each letter, no mistake is possible. Contrast this with English. Miss Soames gives twenty-one ways of writing the same sound. Here they are:

ate	great	feign
bass	eh!	weigh
pain	gaol	aye
pay	gauge	obeyed
dahlia	champagne	weighed
vein	campaign	trait
they	straight	halfpenny †

(Compare eye, lie, high, etc.)

In Esperanto this sound is expressed only and always by "e." In fact, the language is absolutely and entirely phonetic, as all real language was once.

As regards difficulties of vocabulary, the same may be said as in the case of the sounds. Esperanto only adopts the minimum of roots essential, and these are simple, non-ambiguous, and as international as possible. Owing to the device of word-building by means of a few suffixes and prefixes with fixed meaning, the number of roots necessary is very greatly less than in any natural language. ‡

As for difficulties of structure, some of the chief ones are as follows:

Multiplicity and complexity of inflections. This does not exist in Esperanto.

---

* The converse—"one sound, one letter"—is also true, except that the same sound is expressed by *c* and *ts*. (See Appendix C.)

† Prof. Skeat adds a twenty-second: Lord Reay!

‡ Most of these roots are already known to educated people. For the young the learning of a certain number of words presents practically no difficulty; it is in the practical application of words learnt that they break down, and this failure is almost entirely due to "unnecessary" difficulties.

Irregularities and exceptions of all kinds. None in Esperanto.

Complications of orthography. None in Esperanto.

Different senses of same word, and different words used in same sense. Esperanto—" one word, one meaning."

Arbitrary and fluctuating idioms. Esperanto—none. Common sense and common grammar the only limitation to combination of words.

Complexities of syntax. (Think of the use of the subjunctive and infinitive in all languages : οὐ and μή in Greek ; indirect speech in Latin ; negatives, comparisons, etc., etc., in all languages.) Esperanto—none. Common sense the only guide, and no ambiguity in practice. The perfect limpidity of Esperanto, with no syntactical rules, is a most instructive proof of the conventionality and arbitrariness of the niceties of syntax in national languages. After all, the subjunctive was made for man and not man for the subjunctive.

But readers will say : " It is all very well to show by a comparison of forms that Esperanto *ought* to be much easier than a natural language. But we want facts."

Here are some.

In the last chapter it was mentioned that the present writer first took up Esperanto in October 1905, worked at it at odd times, never spoke it or heard it spoken save once, and was able to follow the proceedings of the Congress of Geneva in August 1906, and talk to all foreigners. From a long experience of smattering in many languages and learning a few thoroughly, he is absolutely convinced that this would have been impossible to him in any national language.

A lady who began Esperanto three weeks before the congress, and studied it in a grammar by herself one hour each day, was able to talk in it with all peoples on very simple subjects, and to follow a considerable amount of the lectures, etc.

Amongst the British folk who attended the congress were many clerks and commercial people, who had merely learnt Esperanto by attending a class or a local group meeting once a week, often

for not many months. They had never been out of England
before, nor learnt any other foreign language. They would have
been utterly at sea if they had attempted to do what they did on
a similar acquaintance with any foreign tongue. But during the
two days spent *en route* in Paris, where the British party was fêted
and shown round by the French Esperantists, on the journey
to Geneva, which English and French made together, on lake
steamboats, at picnics and dinners, etc., etc., here they were,
rattling away with great ease and mutual entertainment. Many
of these came from the North of England, and it was a real eye-
opener, over which easy-going South-Englanders would do well to
ponder, to see what results could be produced by a little energy
and application, building on no previous linguistic training.
The Northern accent was evidently a help in pronouncing the
full-sounding vowels of Esperanto.

One Englishman, who was talking away gaily with the French
samideanoj,* was an Esperantist of one year's standing. He had
happened to be at Boulogne in pursuit of a little combined French
and seasiding at the time of the first congress held there, 1905.
One day he got his tongue badly tied up in a café, and was helped
out of his linguistic difficulties with the waiter by certain compatriots, who wore green stars in their buttonholes,† and sat at
another table conversing in an unknown lingo with a crowd of
foreigners. He made inquiries, and found it was Esperanto they
were talking. He was so much struck by their facility, and the
practical way in which they had set his business to rights in a
minute (the waiter was an Esperantist trained *ad hoc*!), that he
decided to give up French and go in for Esperanto. This man
was a real learner of French, who had spent a long time on it,
and realized with disgust his impotence to wield it practically.
To judge by his conversation next year at Geneva, he had no
such difficulty with Esperanto. He was quite jubilant over the
change.

* Terse Esperanto word. = partisans of the same idea (i.e. Esperanto).
† The Esperanto badge.

Such examples could be multiplied *ad infinitum*. No one who attended a congress could fail to be convinced.

Scientific comparison of the respective difficulty of Esperanto and other languages, based on properly collected and tabulated results, does not seem to be yet obtainable. It is difficult to get high-class schools, where language-teaching is a regular and important part of the curriculum, to give an artificial language a fair trial. Properly organized and carried-out tests are greatly to be desired. If and when they are made, it will probably be found that Esperanto is not only very easy of acquisition itself, but that it has a beneficial effect upon other language-learning.*

Meantime, the present writer has carried out one small experiment in a good secondary school for girls, where French and German are regularly spoken and taught for many hours in the week. The head-mistress introduced Esperanto as a regular school subject at the beginning of the Easter term, January 1907. At the end of term a test paper was set, consisting of English sentences to be rendered into French and Esperanto without any dictionary or other aid, and one short passage of English prose to be rendered into both languages with any aid from books that the pupils wished. The object was to determine how far a few hours' teaching of Esperanto would produce results comparable with those obtained in a language learnt for years.

The examinees ranged from fourteen to sixteen years. They had been learning French from two to seven years, and had a daily French lesson, besides speaking French on alternate days in the school. They had learnt Esperanto for ten weeks, from one to one and a half hours per week. *Taking the papers all through, the Esperanto results were nearly as good as the French.*

One last experiment may be mentioned. It was made under scientific conditions on September 23, 1905. The subject was an adult, who had learnt French and German for years at school, and had since taught French to young boys, but was not a linguist by training or education, having read mathematics at the university.

* See pp. 145-55.

He had had no lessons in Esperanto, and had never studied the language, his sole knowledge of it being derived from general conversation with an enthusiast, who had just returned from the Geneva Congress. He was disposed to laugh at Esperanto, but was persuaded to test its possibilities as a language that can be written intelligibly by an educated person merely from dictionary by a few rules.

He was given a page of carefully prepared English to translate into Esperanto. The following written aids were given :

1. Twenty-five crude roots (e.g. *lern-* = to learn.)
2. One suffix, with explanation of its use.
3. A one-page complete grammar of the Esperanto language.
4. An Esperanto-English and an English-Esperanto dictionary.

He produced a good page of perfectly intelligible Esperanto, quite free from serious grammatical mistake. He admitted that he could not translate the passage so well into French or German.

Such experiments go a good way towards proving the case for an artificial language. More are urgently needed, especially of the last two types. They serve to convince all those who come within range of the experiment that an artificial language is a serious project, and may confer great benefits at small cost. Any one can make them with a little trouble, if he can secure a victim. A particularly interesting one is to send a letter in Esperanto to some English or foreign correspondent, enclosing a penny key. The letter will certainly be understood, and very likely the answer will be in Esperanto.

Doubters as to the ease and efficacy of a universal language are not asked to believe without trial. They are merely asked not to condemn or be unfavourable until they have a right to an opinion on the subject. And they are asked to *form* an opinion by personally testing, or at any rate by weighing actual facts. "A fair field and no favour."

The very best way of testing the thing is to study the language for a few hours and attend a congress. The next congress is to be held in Cambridge, England, in August 1907.

Nothing is more unscientific or unintelligent than to scoff at a thing, while refusing to examine whether there is anything in it.

V

THE QUESTION OF PRACTICE (*continued*)—THE INTRODUCTION OF AN INTERNATIONAL LANGUAGE WOULD NOT CAUSE DISLOCATION

IN Chapters II., III., and IV. it was sought to prove that a universal language is desirable in principle, that it already exists and is efficient, and that it is very easy. If these propositions are true, the only valid argument against introducing it at once would be a demonstration that its introduction is either impracticable or else attended with such disadvantages as to outweigh the beneficial results.

Now, it is quite true that certain schemes tending towards international uniformity of practice and, therefore, ultimately productive of saving of labour are nevertheless such that their realization would cause an almost prohibitive dislocation of present organization. A conspicuous example is the proposed adoption of the decimal system in coinage and weights and measures. So great is the loss of time and trouble (and therefore of money) entailed by using an antiquated and cumbrous system instead of a simple and modern one that does the work as well, that the big firm Kynochs some months ago introduced the decimal system, in spite of the enormous difficulty of having to keep a double method going. But hitherto, at any rate, the great disturbance to business that the change would cause has prevented it from being generally made. Both this matter and the curiously out-of-date * system of spelling modern English present a fairly

---

* Out of date, because it has failed to keep pace with the change of pronunciation. Spelling, i.e. use of writing, was merely a device for representing to the eye the spoken sounds, so that failure to do this means getting out of date.

close analogy to the multilingual system of international intercourse, as regards unprofitable expenditure of time and trouble.

But where the analogy breaks down altogether is in the matter of obstacles to reform.

Supposing that all the ministries of education in the world issued orders, that as from January 1, 1909, an auxiliary language should be taught in every government school ; supposing that merchants took to doing foreign business wholesale in an auxiliary language, or that men of science took to issuing all their books and treatises in it ; whose business would be dislocated ? What literature or books would become obsolete ? Who, except foreign correspondence clerks and interpreters, would be a penny the worse ? Surely a useful reform need not be delayed or refused in the interests of interpreters and correspondence clerks. Even these would only be eliminated gradually as the reform spread. There would be absolutely no general confusion analogous to that following on a sudden change to phonetic spelling or the metric system, because nothing would be displaced.

Look at the precedents—the adoption of an international maritime code, and of an international system of cataloguing which puts bibliography on an equal footing all over the world by means of a common system of classification. Did any confusion or dislocation follow on these reforms ? Quite the contrary. It was enough for England and France to agree on the use of the maritime code, and the rest of the nations had to come into line. It would be the same with the official recognition by a group of powerful nations of an auxiliary language. As soon as the world recognizes that it is a labour-saving device on a large scale, and a matter of public convenience on the same plane as codes, telegraphy, or shorthand, it will no doubt be introduced. But why wait until there are rival schemes with large followings and vested interests—in short, until the same obstacles arise to the choice of an international, artificial, and neutral language, as now prevent the elevation of any national language into a universal medium ? The plea of impracticability on the score of dislocation

might then be valid. At present it is not. To have an easy
language that will carry you anywhere and enable you to read
anything, it is sufficient to wish for it. Only, as we Britons are
being taught to "think imperially," so must the nations learn in
this matter to *wish internationally*.

VI

INTERNATIONAL ACTION ALREADY TAKEN FOR THE INTRODUCTION OF AN AUXILIARY LANGUAGE

THE main work of educating the public to "wish internationally,"
the necessary precedent to official action, has naturally in the past
been done by the adherents of the various language-schemes
themselves. An outline of the most important of these movements
is given in the second part of this book.

But apart from these there is now an international organization
that is working for the adoption of an international auxiliary
language, and a brief account of it may be given here.

During the Paris Exhibition of 1900 a number of international
congresses and learned societies, which were holding meetings
there, appointed delegates for the consideration of the international language question. These delegates met on January 17,
1901, and founded a "Delegation for the Adoption of an
International Auxiliary Language." They drew up the following
declaration, which has been approved by all subsequently elected
delegates :

DELEGATION FOR THE ADOPTION OF AN INTERNATIONAL AUXILIARY LANGUAGE

Declaration

The undersigned, deputed by various Congresses and Societies
to study the question of an international auxiliary language, have
agreed on the following points :

(1) There is a necessity to choose and to spread the use of an international language, designed not to replace national idioms in the individual life of each people, but to serve in the written and oral relations between persons whose mother-tongues are different.

(2) In order to fulfil its purpose usefully, an international language must satisfy the following conditions :

> 1st Condition : It must fulfil the needs of the ordinary intercourse of social life, of commercial communications, and of scientific and philosophic relations ;

> 2nd Condition : It must be easily acquired by every person of average elementary education, and especially by persons of European civilization :

> 3rd Condition : It must not be one of the national languages.

(3) It is desirable to organize a general DELEGATION representing all who realize the necessity, as well as the possibility, of an international auxiliary language, and who are interested in its employment. This Delegation will appoint a Committee of members who can meet during a certain period of time. The purpose of this Committee is defined in the following articles.

(4) The choice of the auxiliary language belongs in the first instance to the *International Association of Academies*, or, in case of failure, to the Committee mentioned in Art. 3.

(5) Consequently the first duty of the Committee will be to present to the *International Association of Academies*, in the required forms, the desires expressed by the constituent Societies and Congresses, and to invite it respectfully to realize the project of an auxiliary language.

(6) It will be the duty of the Committee to create a Society for propaganda, to spread the use of the auxiliary language which is chosen.

(7) The undersigned, being delegated by various Congresses and Societies, decide to approach all learned bodies, and all societies of business men and tourists, in order to obtain their adhesion to the present project.

(8) Representatives of regularly constituted Societies which have agreed to the present *Declaration* will be admitted as members of the DELEGATION.

This declaration is the official programme of the Delegation. The most important point of principle to note is Art. 2, 3rd Con. : " It must not be one of the national languages."

As regards the methods of action prescribed, no attempt is to be made to bring direct pressure to bear upon any government. It was rightly felt that the adoption of a universal language is a matter for private initiative. No government can properly take up the question, no Ministry of Education can officially introduce an auxiliary language into the schools under its control, until the principle has met with a certain amount of general recognition. The result of a direct appeal to any government or governments could only have been, in the most favourable case, the appointment by the government appealed to of a commission to investigate and report on the question. Such a commission would examine experts and witnesses from representative bodies, such as academies, institutes, philological and other learned societies. The best course of action, therefore, for the promoters of an international language is to apply direct to such bodies, to bring the question before them and try to gain their support. This is what the Delegation has done.

Now, there already exists an international organization whose object is to represent and focus the opinion of learned societies in all countries. This is the International Association of Academies, formed in 1900 for the express purpose, according to its statutes, of promoting "scientific enterprises of international interest." The delegates feel that the adoption of an international language comes in the fullest sense within the letter and spirit of this statute. It is, therefore, to this Association that the choice of language is, in the first place, left. (Art. 4.)

The Association meets triennially. At its first meeting (Paris 1901) the question of international language was brought before it by General Sébert, of the French Institute, but too late to be included among the agenda of that meeting. The occasion was important as eliciting an expression of opinion on the part of the signatories to General Sébert's address. These included twenty-five members of the French Institute, one of the most distinguished scientific bodies in the world.

At the second meeting of the Association (London 1904) the Delegation did not officially present the question for discussion, but the following paragraph appears in the report of the proceedings of the Royal Society, which was the host (*London Royal Society*, 1904, C. Section of Letters, Thursday, May 26, 1904, p. 33):

"In the course of the sitting, the chairman (Lord Reay, President of the British Academy) submitted to the meeting whether the question of the 'International Auxiliary Language' should be considered, though not included in the agenda. From many quarters applications had been made that the subject might be discussed in some form or other. Prof. Goldziher and M. Perrot spoke against the suggested discussion, the former maintaining that the matter was a general question of international communication, and did not specifically affect scientific interests; the latter announced that he had been commissioned by the *Académie des Inscriptions* to oppose the consideration of this subject. The matter then dropped."

The third meeting of the Association of Academies was held at Vienna at the end of May 1907, under the auspices of the Vienna Academy of Science. The question was officially laid before it by the Delegation. The Association declared, for formal reasons, that the question did not fall within its competence.*

Up till now only two national academies have shown themselves favourable to the scheme, those of Vienna and Copenhagen.

---

* In the voting as to the inclusion of the question in the agenda, eight votes were cast in favour of international language, and twelve against. This considerable minority shows very encouraging progress in such a body, considering the newness of the scheme.

The Vienna Academy commissioned one of its most eminent members, Prof. Schuchardt, to watch the movement on its behalf, and to keep it informed on the subject. In 1904 he presented a report favourable to an international language. He and Prof. Jespersen are amongst the most famous philologists who support the movement.

It is not therefore anticipated that the Association of Academies will take up the question ; and the Delegation, thinking it desirable not to wait indefinitely till it is converted, has proceeded to the election of a committee, as provided in Art. 4 of the Declaration. It consists of twelve members, with powers to add to their number. It will meet in Paris, October 5, 1907. It is anticipated that the language chosen will be Esperanto. None of the members of this international committee are English, all the English savants invited having declined.

What may be the practical effect of the choice made by this Committee remains to be seen. In France there is a permanent Parliamentary Commission for the consideration of questions affecting public education. This Commission has for some time had before it a proposal for the introduction of Esperanto into the State schools of France, signed by twelve members of Parliament and referred by the House to the Commission. This year the proposal has been presented again in a different form. The text of the scheme, which is much more practical than the former one, is as follows :

"The study of the international language Esperanto will be included in the curricula of those government schools in which modern languages are already taught.

"This study will be optional, and candidates who offer for the various examinations English, German, Italian, Spanish, or Arabic, will be allowed to offer Esperanto as an additional subject.

"They will be entitled to the advantages enjoyed by candidates who offer an additional language."

At present it is a very usual thing to offer an additional language, and if this project passes, Esperanto will be on exactly the same footing as other languages for this purpose. The project of recognizing Esperanto as a principal language for examination was entirely impracticable. It is far too easy, and would merely have become a "soft option" and a refuge for the destitute.

It is said that a majority of the Commission are in favour of introducing an auxiliary language into the schools, when one has been chosen by the Delegation or by the Association of Academies. It is therefore possible that in a year or two Esperanto may be officially recognized in France; and if this is so, other nations will have to examine the matter seriously.

Considering that the French are notoriously bad linguists and, above all other peoples, devoted to the cult of their own language and literature, it is somewhat remarkable that the cause of an artificial language should have made more progress among them than elsewhere. It might have been anticipated that the obstructionist outcry, raised so freely in all countries by those who imagine that an insidious attack is being made on taste, culture, and national language and literature, would have been particularly loud in France. On the contrary, it is precisely in that country that the movement has made most popular progress, and that it numbers the most scientists, scholars, and distinguished men among its adherents. Is it that history will one day have to record another case of France leading Europe in the van of progress?

Encouraged by the number of distinguished signatures obtained in France to their petition in 1901, the Delegation drew up a formula of assent to their Declaration, which they circulate amongst (1) members of academies, (2) members of universities, in all countries. They also keep a list of societies of all kinds who have declared their adherence to the scheme. The latest lists (February and March 1907) show 1,060 signatures of academicians and university members, and 273 societies. In both cases the most influential backing is in France. Thus among the signatures figure in Paris alone:

　　10 professors of the Collège de France ;
　　　8　　,,　　　,,　　,, Faculty of Medicine ;
　　13　　,,　　　,,　　,, Faculty of Science ;
　　11　　,,　　　,,　　,, Faculty of Letters ;
　　12　　,,　　　,,　　,, École Normale ;
　　37 members of the Academy of Science ;

besides a host of other members of various learned bodies. Many of these are members of that august body the Institut de France, and one is a member of the Académie française— M. Lavisse.

It is the same in the other French Universities : Lyons University, 53 professors ; Dijon, 34 ; Caen, 18 ; Besançon, 15 ; Grenoble, 26 ; Marseilles, 56, and so on.

Universities in other lands make a fair showing. America contributes supporters from John Hopkins University, 20 professors ; Boston Academy of Arts and Sciences, 13 members ; Harvard, 7 professors ; Columbia University, 23 professors ; Washington Academy of Science, 19 members ; Columbus University, Ohio, 21 professors, etc. Dublin and Edinburgh both contribute a few. England is represented by one entry : " Cambridge, 2 professors." Perhaps the Cambridge Congress will change this somewhat. It will be strange if any one can actually witness a congress without having his imagination to some extent stirred by the possibilities.

A noticeable feature of the action of the Delegation throughout has been the scientific spirit in which it has gone to work, and its absolute impartiality as to the language to be adopted. It has everywhere, in its propaganda and circulars, spoken of " an international auxiliary language," and has been careful not to prejudge in any way the question as to which shall be adopted.

It may be news to many that there are several rival languages in the field. Even the enthusiastic partisans of Esperanto are often completely ignorant of the existence of competitors. It was partly with the object of furnishing full information to the

Delegates who are to make the choice, that MM. Couturat and Leau composed their admirable *Histoire de la langue universelle.* It contains a brief but scientific account of each language mentioned, the leading principles of its construction, and an excellent critique. The main principles are disengaged by the authors with a masterly clearness and precision of analysis from the mass of material before them. Though they are careful to express no personal preference, and let fall nothing which might unfairly prejudice the delegates in favour of any scheme, it is not difficult to judge, by a comparison of the scientific critiques, which of the competing schemes analysed most fully carries out the principles which experience now shows to be essential to success for any artificial language.

The impression left is, that whether judged by the test of conformity to necessary principles, or by the old maxim " possession is nine points of the law," Esperanto has no serious rival.

VII

CAN THE INTERNATIONAL LANGUAGE BE LATIN?

THERE are some who fully admit the desirability of an international language, but say that we have no need to invent one, as we have Latin. This tends to be the argument of literary persons.* They back it up by pointing out that Latin has already done duty in the Middle Ages as a common medium, and therefore, they say, what it has once done with success it can do again.

It is hard to argue with such persons, because they have not grasped the fact that the nature of international communication has undergone a complete change, and that therefore there is no

---

* It has even cropped up again in the able articles in *The Times* on the reformed pronunciation of Latin (April 1907).

presumption that the same medium will suffice for carrying it on. In the Middle Ages the cosmopolitan public was almost entirely a learned one. The only people who wanted to communicate with foreigners (except for a certain amount of commerce) were scholars, and the only things they wanted to communicate about were learned subjects, mostly of a philosophical or literary nature, which Latin was adapted to express. The educated public was extremely small, and foreign travel altogether beyond the reach of all but the very few. The overwhelming mass of the people were illiterate, and fast tied to their native spot by lack of pence, lack of communications, and the general conditions of life.

Now that everybody can read and write and get about, and all the conditions of life have changed, the cosmopolitan public, so far from being confined to a handful of scholars and merchants, extends down to and is largely made up of that terrible modern production, "the man in the street." It is quite ridiculous to pretend that because an Erasmus or a Casaubon could carry on literary controversies, with amazing fluency and hard-hitting, in Ciceronian Latin, therefore " the bald-headed man at the back of the omnibus " can give up the time necessary to obtaining a control of Latin sufficient for the conduct of his affairs, or for hobnobbing with his kind abroad.

It is waste of time to argue with those who do not realize that the absolute essentials of any auxiliary language in these days are ease of acquirement and accessibility to all. There are actually some newspapers published in Latin and dealing with modern topics. As an amusement for the learned they are all very well; but the portentous periphrases to which they are reduced in describing tramway accidents or motor-cars, the rank obscurity of the terms in which advertisements of the most ordinary goods are veiled, ought to be enough to drive their illusions out of the heads of the modern champions of Latin for practical purposes. Let these persons take in the Roman *Vox Urbis* for a month or two, or get hold of a copy of the London *Alaudae*, and see how they feel then.

A dim perception of the requirements of the modern world has inspired the various schemes for a barbarized and simplified Latin. It is almost incredible that the authors of such schemes cannot see that debased Latin suffers from all the defects alleged against an artificial language, plus quite prohibitory ones of its own, without attaining the corresponding advantages. It is just as artificial as an entirely new language, without being nearly so easy (especially to speak) or adaptable to modern life. It sins against the cardinal principle that an auxiliary language shall inflict no damage upon any natural one. In short, it disgusts both parties (scholars and tradesmen), and satisfies the requirements of neither. Those who want an easy language, within the reach of the intelligent person with only an elementary school groundwork of education, don't get it; and the scholarly party, who treat any artificial language as a cheap commercial scheme, have their teeth set on edge by unparalleled barbarisms, which must militate most seriously against the correct use of classical Latin.

Such schemes are dead of their own dogginess.

Latin, pure or mongrel, won't do.

VIII

CAN THE INTERNATIONAL LANGUAGE BE GREEK?

THIS chapter might be as short and dogmatic as Mark Twain's celebrated chapter upon snakes in Ireland. It would be enough to merely answer " No," but that the indefatigable Mr. Henderson, after running through three artificial languages of his own, has come to the conclusion that Greek is the thing. Certainly, as regards flexibility and power of word-formation, Greek would be better than Latin on its own merits. But it is too hard, and the scheme has nothing practical about it.

IX

CAN THE INTERNATIONAL LANGUAGE BE A MODERN LANGUAGE?

JINGOES are not wanting who say that it is unpatriotic of any Englishman to be a party to the introduction of a neutral language, because English is manifestly destined to be the language of the world.

Reader, did you ever indulge in the mild witticism of asking a foreigner where the English are mentioned in the Bible? The answer, of course, is, *The meek shall inherit the earth.* But if the foreigner is bigger than you, don't tell him until you have got to a safe distance.

It is this attitude of self-assertion, coupled with the tacit assumption that the others don't count much, that makes the English so detested on the Continent. It is well reflected in the claim to have their own language adopted as a common means of communication between all other peoples.

This claim is not put forward in any spirit of deliberate insolence, or with the intention of ignoring other people's feelings; though the very unconsciousness of any arrogance in such an attitude really renders it more galling, on account of the tacit conclusion involved therein. It is merely the outcome of ignorance and of that want of tact which consists of inability to put oneself at the point of view of others. The interests of English-speaking peoples are enormous, far greater than those of any other group of nations united by a common bond of speech. But it is a form of narrow provincial ignorance to refuse on that account to recognize that, compared to the whole bulk of civilized people, the English speakers are in a small minority, and that the majority includes many high-spirited peoples with a strongly developed sense of nationality, and destined to play a very important part in the history of the world. Any sort of movement to have English or any other national language adopted officially as a universal auxiliary language would at once entail a boycott of the favoured language on the part of a ring of other powerful nations, who could not afford to give a rival the benefit of this augmented prestige. And it is precisely upon universality of adoption that the great use of an international language will depend.

To sum up : the ignorance of contemporary history and fact displayed in the suggestion of giving the preference to any national language is only equalled by its futility, for it *is* futile to put forward a scheme that has no chance of even being discussed internationally as a matter of practical politics.

A proof is that precisely the same objection to an auxiliary language is raised in France—namely, that it is unpatriotic, because it would displace French from that proud position.

The above remarks will be wholly misunderstood if they are taken to imply any spirit of Little Englandism on the part of the writer. On the contrary, he is ardently convinced of the mighty *rôle* that will be played among the nations by the British Empire, and has had much good reason in going to and fro in the world to ponder on its unique achievement in the past. When fully organized on some terms of partnership as demanded by the growth of the Colonies, it will go even farther in the future. But all this has nothing to do with an international language. Howsoever mighty, the British Empire will not swallow up the earth—at any rate, not in our time. And till it does, it is not practical politics to expect other peoples to recognize English as the international language as between themselves.

There are, in fact, two quite separate questions :

(1) Supposing it is possible for any national language to become the international one, which has the best claims?

(2) Is it possible for any national language to be adopted as the international one?

To question (1) the answer undoubtedly is " English." It is already the language of the sea, and to a large extent the medium for transacting business between Europeans and Asiatic races, or between the Asiatic races themselves.*　Moreover, except for its pronunciation and spelling, it has intrinsically the best claim, as being the furthest advanced along the common line of development of Aryan language.†　But the discussion of this question has no more than an academic interest, because the answer to question (2) is, for political reasons, in the negative.

X

CAN THE EVOLUTION OF AN INTERNATIONAL LANGUAGE BE LEFT TO THE PROCESS OF NATURAL SELECTION BY FREE COMPETITION?

"You base your argument for an international language mainly on the operation of economical laws.　Be consistent, then; leave the matter to Nature.　By unlimited competition the best language is bound to be evolved and come to the top in the struggle for life.　Let the fittest survive, and don't bother about Esperanto."

On a first hearing this sounds fairly plausible, yet it is honeycombed with error.

In the first place, it proves too much.　The same argument could be adduced for the abandonment of effort of all kind whatever to improve upon Nature and her processes.　"You can walk and run and swim.　Don't bother to invent boats and bicycles, trains and aeroplanes, that will bring you more into touch with other peoples.　Let Nature evolve the best form of international locomotion."

Again, Nature does not tend towards uniformity.　She produces an infinity of variety in the individual, and out of this variety she selects and evolves certain prevailing types.　But these types

---

* Another argument is that based on the comparative numbers of people who speak the principal European languages as their mother-tongue.　No accurate statistics exist, but an interesting estimate is quoted by Couturat and Leau (*Hist. de la langue universelle*), which puts English first with about 120,000,000, followed at a distance of 30,000,000 or 40,000,000 by Russian.

† This is explained in Part III., chap. i., *q.v.*

differ widely within the limits of the world under varying conditions of environment. What we are seeking to establish is world-wide uniformity, in spite of difference of environment.

Again, the argument confuses a sub-characteristic with an organism. A language is not an organism, but one of the characteristics of man. After the lapse of countless ages there are grey horses and black, bay and chestnut, presumably because greyness and blackness and the rest are incidental characteristics of a horse. No one of them gives him a greater advantage than the others in his struggle for life, or helps him particularly to perform the functions of horsiness.

Just in the same way a man may be equally well equipped with all the qualities that make for success, whether he speaks English or French, Russian or Japanese. It cannot be shown that language materially helps one people as against another, or even that the best race evolves the best language.* Take the last mentioned. If there is one people on the face of the globe who rejoice in an impossible language, it is the Japanese. In the early days of foreign intercourse a good Jesuit father reported that the Japanese were courteous and polite to strangers, but their language was plainly the invention of the devil. To a modern mind the language may have outlived its putative father, but its reputation has not improved, so far as ease is concerned. Yet who will say that it has impaired national efficiency?

The fact is, that for purposes of transaction of ordinary affairs by those who speak it as a mother tongue, one language is about as good as another. Whether it survives or spreads depends, not upon its intrinsic qualities as a language, but upon the success of the race that speaks it.† There is, therefore, no

* Greece went down before Rome. Which was the better race, meaning by "better" the more capable of imposing its language and manners on the world? Yet who doubts that Greek was the better language?

† A curious phenomenon of our day suggests a possible partial exception. In Switzerland French is steadily encroaching and bearing back German. Is this owing to the intrinsic qualities of French language and civilization? Materially, the Germans have the greater expansive power.

presumption that the best or the most suitable or the easiest language will spread over the world by its own merits, or even that any easy or regular language will be evolved. Printing and education have altogether arrested the natural process of evolution of language on the lips of men. This is one justification for the application of new artificial reforms to language and spelling, which tend no longer to move naturally with the times as heretofore.

As regards free competition between rival artificial languages, the same considerations hold good. The worse might prevail just as easily as the better, because the determining factor is not the nature of the language, but the influence and general capacity of the rival backers. Of course a very bad or hard artificial language would not prevail against an easy one. But beyond a certain point of ease a universal language cannot go (ease meaning the ease of all), and that limit has probably been about reached now. Between future schemes there will be such a mere fractional difference in respect of ease, that competition becomes altogether beside the point. The thing is to take an easy one and stick to it.

XI

OBJECTIONS TO AN INTERNATIONAL LANGUAGE ON AESTHETIC GROUNDS

ONE of the commonest arguments that advocates of a universal language have to face runs something like this :

"Yes, there really does seem to be something in what you say—your language may save time and money and grease the wheels of business; but, after all, we are not all business men, nor are we all out after dollars. Just think what a dull, drab uniformity your scheme would lay over the lands like a pall. By the artificial removal of natural barriers you are aiding and abetting the vulgarization of the world. You are doing what in you lies to eliminate the racy, the local, the picturesque. The tongues of men are as stately trees, set deep in the black, mouldering soil of the past, and rich with its secular decay. The leaves are the words of the people, old yet ever new, and the flowers are the nation's poems, drawing their life from the thousand tiny roots that twist and twine unseen about the lives and struggles of bygone men. You are calling to us to come forth from the cool seclusion of these trees' shade, to leave their delights and toil in the glare of the world at raising a mushroom growth on a dull, featureless plain that reaches everywhither. Modern Macbeths, sophisticated by your modernity and adding perverted instinct to crime, you are murdering not sleep, but dreams—dreams that haunt about the mouldering lodges of the past, and soften the contact with reality by lending their own colouring atmosphere. You are hammering the last nail into the coffin of the old leisurely past, the past that raised the cathedrals, to which taste and feeling were of supreme moment, and when man put something of himself into his every work."

The man must be indeed dull of soul who cannot join in a dirge for the beauty of the vanishing past. Turn where we may now, we find the same railways, the same trams, music-halls, coats and trousers. The mad rush of modernity with its levelling tendency really is killing off what is quaint, out of the way, and racy of the soil. But why visit the sins of modernity upon an international language? The last sentence of the indictment itself suggests the line of defence. "You are hammering the last nail into the coffin of the old, leisurely past. . . ."

Quite so, you *are*.

The universal ability to use an auxiliary language on occasion rounds off and completes the levelling process. But the old leisurely past will not be any the less dead, or any the less effectually buried, if one nail is not driven home in the coffin. The slayer is modernity at large, made up of science, steam, democracy, universal education, and many other things—but especially universal education. And the verdict can be, at the most, justifiable, or at any rate inevitable, pasticide. You cannot eat your cake and have it; you cannot kill off all the bad things and keep all the good ones. With sterilization goes purification, pasticide may be accompanied by pasteurization. At any rate, "the old order changeth," and you've got to let it change.

The whole history of the "progress" of the world, meaning often material progress, is eloquent of the lesson that it is vain to set artificial limits to advancing invention. The substitution of cheap mechanical processes of manufacture for hand-work involved untold misery to many, and incidentally led to the partial disappearance of a type of character which the world could ill afford to lose, and which we would give much to be able to bring back. The old semi-artist-craftsman, with hand and eye really trained up to something like their highest level of capacity, with knowledge not wide, but deep, and all gained from experience, and not from books or technical education—this type of character is a loss. Many, with the gravest reason, are dissatisfied with the type which has already largely replaced it, and which will replace it for good or evil, but ever more swiftly and surely. But no well-judging person proposes on that account to forgo the material advantages conferred upon mankind by the invention of machinery. If the world rejects, on sentimental grounds, the labour-saving invention of international language, it will be flying in the face of economic history, and it will not appreciably retard the disappearance of the picturesque.

There is another type of argument which may also be classed as aesthetic, but which differs somewhat from the one just discussed. It emanates chiefly from literary men and scholars, and may be presented as follows :

"Language is precious, and worthy of study, inasmuch as it enshrines the imperishable monuments of the thought and genius of the race on whose lips it was born. The study of the words and forms in which a nation clothed its thoughts throws many a ray of light on phases of the evolution of the race itself, which would otherwise have remained dark.   The history of a language and literature is in some measure an epitome of the history of a people.   We miss all these points of interest in your artificial language, and we shall, therefore, refuse to study it, and hereby commit it to the devil."

This is a particularly humiliating type of answer to receive, because it implies that one is an ass.   In truth the man who should invent an artificial language and invite the world to study it for itself would be a fool, and a very swell-headed fool at that. It seems in vain to point this out to persons who use the above argument; or to explain to them that they would be aided in their study of languages that do repay study by the introduction of an easy international language, because many commentaries, etc., would become accessible to them, which are not so now, or only at the expense of deciphering some difficult language in which the commentary is written, the commentary itself being in no sense literature, and its form a matter of complete indifference.

Back comes the old answer in one form or another, every variation tainted with the heresy that the language is to be studied as a language for itself.

Perhaps the least tedious way of giving an idea of this kind of opposition, and the way in which it may be met, is to give some extracts from a scholar's letter, and the writer's answer.   The letter is fairly typical.

" MY DEAR ——,
    "Many thanks for your long letter on Esperanto. . . . According to the books, Esperanto can be learnt quickly by any one.   This means that they will forget it quite as rapidly ; for what is easily acquired is soon forgotten. . . . In my humble opinion, an Englishman who knows French and German would do much better to devote any extra time at his disposal to the study of his own language, which, I repeat, is one of the most delicate mediums of communication now in existence.   It has taken

centuries to construct, while Esperanto was apparently created in a few hours. One is God's handiwork, and the other a man's toy. Personally, any living language interests me more than Esperanto. I am sorry I am such a heretic, but I fear my love for the English language carries me away. . . .

> " Yours ever,
>
> "_____."

The points that rankle are artificiality and lack of a history.

Reply

" MY DEAR ——,

"I really can't put it any more plainly, so I must just repeat it : we are not trying to introduce a language that has any interest for anybody in itself. An international language is a labour-saving device. The question is, Is it an efficient one ? If so, it must surely be adopted. The world wants to be saved labour. It never pays permanently to do things a longer way, if the shorter one produces equally good results. No one has yet proved, or, in my opinion, advanced any decent argument tending to show, that the results produced by a universal language will not be just as good *for many purposes* * as those produced by national languages. That the results are more economically produced surely does not admit of doubt.

" 'Personally, any living language interests me more than Esperanto.' Of course it does. So it does me, and most sensible people. But what the digamma does it matter to Esperanto whether we are interested in it or not ? It is not there to interest us. The question is, Does it, or not, save us or others unprofitable labour on a large scale ? Neither you nor most sane persons are probably particularly interested in short-hand or Morse codes or any signalling systems. Yet they bear up.

* And those very important ones, relatively to man's whole field of activity.

"Do try to see that we think there is a certain felt want, amongst countless numbers of persons, which is much more efficiently and economically met by a neutral, easy, international language, than by any national one. That is the position you have got to controvert, if you are seriously to weaken the argument in favour of an international language. If you say that it is not a want felt by many people, I can only say, at the risk of being dogmatic, that you are wrong. I happen to know that it is.* The question then is, Is there an easy way of meeting that want? And the equally certain and well-grounded answer is, There is. . . .

"As to your argument that what is easy is more easily forgotten —it is true. But I think you must see that, neither in practice nor in principle, does it or should it make for choosing the harder way of arriving at a given result. Chance the forgetting, if necessary re-learning as required, and use the time and effort saved for some more remunerative purpose.

"'One is God's handiwork, the other a man's toy.' I should have said the first was man's lip-work, but I see what you mean. It is God working through his creature's natural development. The same is equally true of all man's 'toys.' Man moulded his language in pursuance of his ends under God. Under the same guidance he moulded the steam engine, the typewriter, shorthand, the semaphore, and all kinds of signals. What are the philosophical *differentia* that make Esperanto a toy, and natural language God's handiwork? Apparently the fact that Esperanto is 'artificial,' i.e. consciously produced by art. If this is the criterion, beware lest you damn man's works wholesale. If this is not the criterion, what is?

* I have before me a list of 119 societies, representing many different lines of work and play and many nations, who had already in 1903 given in their adhesion to a scheme for an international language. Technical terms alone (in all departments of study) want standardizing, and an international language affords the best means. The number of societies is now (1907) over 270.

" 'An Englishman who knows French and German would do much better to devote any extra time at his disposal to the study of his own language.' Yes—if his object is to qualify as an artist in language. No—if his object is to save time and trouble in communicating with foreigners. You must compare like with like. It is unscientific and a confusion of thought to change the subject-matter of a man's employment of his time on grounds other than those fairly intercomparable. You have dictated as to how a man should employ his time by changing his object in employing his time. This makes the whole discussion irrelevant, in so far as it deals with the comparative advantage of studying one language or the other.

"Time's up! I have missed my after-lunch walk, and I expect only hardened your heart.

" Yours,

" ————."

And I had !

XII

WILL AN INTERNATIONAL LANGUAGE DISCOURAGE THE STUDY OF MODERN LANGUAGES, AND THUS BE DETRIMENTAL TO CULTURE ?—PARALLEL WITH THE QUESTION OF COMPULSORY GREEK

THERE is a broad, twofold distinction in the aims with which the study of foreign languages is organized and undertaken.

It serves : first, purely utilitarian ends, and is a means; secondly, the purposes of culture, and is an end in itself.

An international auxiliary language aims at supplanting the first type of study completely, and, as it claims, with profit to the students. The second type it hopes to leave wholly intact, and disclaims any attempt to interfere with it in any way. How far is this possible ?

The answer depends mainly upon the efficiency of the alternative offered by the new-comer in each case as a possible substitute.

Firstly, if it is true that a great portion of the human race, especially in the big polyglot empires and the smaller states of Europe, are groaning under the incubus of the language difficulty, and have to spend years on the study of mere words before they can fit themselves for an active career, then the abolition of this heavy handicap on due preparation for each man's proper business in life will liberate much time for more profitable studies. It is certain that the majority of mankind are non-linguistic by nature and inclination rather than linguistic—i.e. that the best chance of developing their natural capacities to the utmost and making them useful and agreeable members of society does not lie in making all alike swallow an overdose of foreign languages during the acquisitive years of youth. By doing so, vast waste is caused, taking the world round. As to the attainment of the object of this first type of language study, not only is it as efficiently secured by a single universal language, but far more so. *Ex hypothesi* the object is utilitarian; the language is a means. Well, a universal language is a better means than a national one—first, because, being universal, it is a means to more; secondly, because, being easy and one, it is a means that more people can grasp and employ. In fact, it is in this field an efficient substitute; it saves much, without losing anything.

For the second type of language-study, on the other hand, where the end is culture and the language is studied for itself and in no wise as an indifferent means, a universal artificial language offers no substitute at all. This end is not on its programme. Why, then, should any language-study that is organized in view of culture be given up on its account?

It may, of course, be said that the time given to it by those who pursue culture in language will be taken from the time devoted to more worthy linguistic study, and will therefore prejudice the learning of other languages. This is a point of technical pedagogics or psychology. There is very good reason, from the standpoint of these sciences, to believe that a study of a simple *type-tongue* would, on the contrary, pay for itself in increased facility in learning other languages. But this is more fully discussed in the chapter for teachers (see pp. 145-55).

The question, however, is not in reality quite so simple as this. There is no water-tight partition between utilitarian and cultural language-study. They act and react upon each other. There really is some ground for anxiety, lest the provision of facilities for learning an easy artificial language at your door may prevent people from going out of their way to learn national ones, which would have awakened scholarly instincts in them. The cause of culture would thus sustain some real hurt.

The question is another phase—a wider and lower-grade phase —of the great compulsory Greek question at Oxford and Cambridge. It affects the masses, whereas the Greek controversy affects the few at the top; but otherwise the issue at stake is essentially the same.

In both cases the bedrock of the problem is this, Can we afford to put the many through a grind, which is on the whole unprofitable to them and does not attain its object of conferring culture, in order to uphold the traditional system in the interests of the few? In neither case do the reformers desire to suppress the study of the old culture-giving language ; rather it is hoped that the interests of scholarly and liberal learning will benefit by being freed from the dead weight of grammar grinders, whose mechanical performance and monkey antics are merely a dodge to catch a copper from the examiners.

When Greek is no longer bolstered up by the protection of compulsion, some of the present bounty-fed (i.e. compulsion-fed) facilities for its study will no doubt disappear from the schools which are at present forced to provide them. With them will be lost some recruits who would have been led by the facilities to study Greek, and would have studied it to their profit. On the other hand, the university will be open to numbers of students who are at present shut out by the Greek tariff. Another barrier against modernity will go down, and democracy make another step out of the proverbial gutter towards the university.

Similarly, the possession of a universally understood medium of communication will in some cases deter people from making the effort to study real language, with all the treasures of original literature to which it is the key.

> 'Tis true, 'tis pity; and pity 'tis, 'tis true.

But—and this is the great point—it will open the cosmopolitan outlook to countless thousands who could never hope to grapple successfully with even one national language. This cannot be a small gain.

It all comes back to this—you cannot eat your cake and have it too. *Il faut souffrir pour être belle.* The international language has the defects of its qualities. But then its qualities are great, and the world is their sphere of utility.

XIII

OBJECTION TO AN INTERNATIONAL LANGUAGE ON THE GROUND THAT IT WILL SOON SPLIT UP INTO DIALECTS

THIS is a particularly unfortunate objection, because it displays a radical ignorance of the history of language, and of the conditions under which it develops.

In the first place, the whole tendency of language in the modern world is towards disappearance of local dialects, and their absorption into a uniform literary language. The dialects of England are almost dead before the onset of universal education, and the great work of Dr. Wright was only just in time to rescue them from oblivion. Even one generation hence it will be impossible to collect much of the local speech recorded in his dictionary. It is the same in Germany and everywhere, though, of course, all countries are not equally advanced in this respect. A standard form of words and grammar is fixed by print for the literary language, and when every one can read and write, it is all up with national evolution of language, such as has produced all national languages. A gradual change of the phonetic value given to the written symbols there may be. This has been pre-eminently the case in England, though even this will now be arrested by universal education. But a change of forms or of grammar can only be indefinitely slight and gradual. When it takes place, it reflects a common advance of the literary language, and not local or dialectical variation (though the common advance may have originally spread from one locality).

In the second place, dialects are variations that spring up under the stress of local circumstance in the familiar every-day unconscious use of a common mother tongue among people of the same race and inhabiting the same district. Now, these are the very circumstances in which an auxiliary international language never can, and never will, be used. The only exception is the case of people meeting together for the conscious practice of the language or using it in jest.

There are no occasions when an international language would be naturally used when any variation from standard usage would not be a distinct disadvantage as tending to unintelligibility. In short, a neutral language consciously learned as a means of communication with strangers is not on an equal footing with, or exposed to the same influences as, a mother tongue used by people every day under like conditions.

A cardinal point of difference is well illustrated by Esperanto. The whole foundation of the language, vocabulary, grammar, and everything else, is contained in one small book of a few pages, called *Fundamento de Esperanto*. No change can be made in this except by a competent elected international authority. Of course, no text-books or grammars will be authorized for the use of any nation that are not in accordance with the *Fundamento*. People will make mistakes, of course, just as they make mistakes in any foreign language, and they can help themselves out with any words from other languages, just as they do now when their

French or German fails them. But the standard is always there, simple and short, to correct any aberration, and there is no room for any alterations in form or structure to creep in.

XIV

OBJECTION THAT THE PRESENT INTERNATIONAL LANGUAGE (ESPERANTO) IS TOO DOGMATIC, AND REFUSES TO PROFIT BY CRITICISM

It is true that Esperantists refuse to make any change in their language at present, and this is found irritating by some able critics, who wrongly imagine that this attitude amounts to a claim of perfection for Esperanto. The matter may be easily put right.

The inadmissibility of change (even for the better) is purely a matter of policy and dictated by practical considerations. Esperantists make no claim to infallibility; they want to see their language universally adopted, and they want to see it as perfect as possible. Actual and bitter experience shows that the international language which admits change is lost. Universal acceptance and present change are incompatible. Esperantists, therefore, bow to the inevitable and deliberately choose to concentrate for the present on acceptance. General acceptance, indeed, while it imposes upon the present body of Esperantists self-restraint in abstaining from change, is in reality the essential condition of profitable future amendment. When an international language has attained the degree of dissemination already enjoyed by Esperanto, the only safe kind of change that can be made is *a posteriori*, not *a priori*. When Esperanto has been officially adopted and comes into wide use, actual experience and consensus of usage amongst its leading writers will indicate the modifications that are ripe for official adoption. The competent international official authority will then from time to time duly register such changes, and they will become officially part of the language.

Till then, any change can only cause confusion and alienate support. No one is going to spend time learning a language which is one thing to-day and another thing to-morrow. When the time comes for change, the authority will only proceed cautiously one step at a time, and its decrees will only set the seal upon that which actual use has hit off.

This, then, is the explanation of the famous adjective "netuŝebla," applied by Dr. Zamenhof to his language, and so much resented in certain quarters. Surely not only is this degree of dogmatism amply justified by practical considerations, but it would amount to positive imprudence on the part of Esperantists to act otherwise. If the inventor of the language can show sufficient self-restraint, after long years spent in touching and retouching his language, to hold his hand at a given point (and he has declared that self-restraint is necessary), surely others need not be hurt at their suggestions not being adopted, even though they may in some cases be real improvements.

The following extracts, translated from the Preface to *Fundamento de Esperanto* (the written basic law of Esperanto), should set the question in the right light. It will be seen that Dr. Zamenhof expressly contemplates the "gradual perfection" (*perfektigado*) of his language, and by no means lays claim to finality or infallibility.

"Having the character of *fundament*, the three works reprinted in this volume must be above all inviolable (*netuŝeblaj*). . . . The fundament must remain inviolable *even with its errors.* . . . Having once lost its strict inviolability, the work would lose its exceptional and necessary character of dogmatic fundamentality; and the user, finding one translation in one edition, and another in another, would have no security that I should not make another change to-morrow, and his confidence and support would be lost.

"To any one who shows me an expression that is not good in the Fundamental book, I shall calmly reply : Yes, it is an error ; but it must remain inviolable, for it belongs to the fundamental

document, in which no one has the right to make any change. . . .
I showed, *in principle*, how the strict inviolability of the *Fundamento* will always preserve the unity of our language, without however preventing the language not only from becoming richer, but even from constantly becoming more perfect. But *in practice* we (for causes already many times explained) must naturally be very cautious in the process of 'perfecting' the language : (*a*) we must not do this light-heartedly, but only in case of absolute necessity ; (*b*) it can only be done (after mature judgment) by some central institution, having indisputable authority for the whole Esperanto world, and not by any private persons. . . .

"Until the time when a central authoritative institution shall decide to *augment* (never to *change*) the existing fundament by rendering official new words or rules, everything good, which is not to be found in the *Fundamento de Esperanto*, is to be regarded not as compulsory, but only as recommended."

XV

SUMMARY OF OBJECTIONS TO AN INTERNATIONAL LANGUAGE

An attempt has been made in the preceding chapters to deal with the more important and obvious arguments put forward by those who will hear nothing of an international language. The objections are, however, so numerous, cover such a wide field, and in some cases are so mutually destructive, that it may be instructive to present them in an orderly classification.

> For there we have them all "at one fell swoop,"
>   Instead of being scattered through the pages ;
> They stand forth marshalled in a handsome troop,
>   To meet the ingenuous youth of future ages.
>   BYRON.

Let us hope that they will die of exposure, like the famous appendix pilloried by Byron, and that the ingenuous one will be able to regard them as literary curiosities.

If the business of an argument is to be unanswerable, the place of honour certainly belongs to the religious argument. Any one who really believes that an international language is an impious attempt to reverse the judgment of Babel will continue firm in his faith, though one speak with the tongues of men and of angels.

Here, then, are the objections, classified according to content.

OBJECTIONS TO AN INTERNATIONAL LANGUAGE

I. *Religious.*

It is doomed to confusion, because it reverses the judgment of Babel.

II. *Aesthetic and sentimental.*

(1) It is a cheap commercial scheme, unworthy of the attention of scholars.

(2) It vulgarizes the world and tends to dull uniformity.

(3) It weakens patriotism by diluting national spirit with cosmopolitanism.

(4) It has no history, no link with the past.

(5) It is artificial, which is a sin in itself.

III. *Political.*

(1) It is against English [Frenchmen read " French "] interests, as diverting prestige from the national tongue.

(2) It is socialistic and even anarchical in tendency, and will facilitate the operations of the international disturbers of society.

IV. *Literary and linguistic.*

(1) Lacking history and associations, it is unpoetical and unsuited to render the finer shades of thought and feeling. It will, therefore, degrade and distort the monuments of national literatures which may be translated into it.

(2) It may even discourage authors, ambitious of a wide public, from writing in their own tongue. Original works in the artificial

language can never have the fine savour of a master's use of his mother tongue.

(3) Its precisely formal and logical vocabulary and construction debauches the literary sense for the niceties of expression. Therefore, even if not used as a substitute for the mother tongue, its concurrent use, which will be thrust on everybody, will weaken the best work in native idioms.

(4) It will split up into dialects.

(5) Pronunciation will vary so as to be unintelligible.

(6) It is too dogmatic, and refuses to profit by criticism.

V. *Educational and cultural.*

(1) It will prejudice the study of modern languages.

(2) It will provide a " soft option " for examinees.

VI. *Personal and particular.*

It is prejudicial to the vested interests of modern language teachers, foreign correspondence clerks, interpreters, multilingual waiters and hotel porters.

VII. *Technical.*

This heading includes the criticisms in detail of various schemes—e.g. it is urged against Esperanto that its accent is monotonous; that its accusative case is unnecessary; that its principle of word-formation from roots is not strictly logical; that its vocabulary is too Romance; that its vocabulary is not Romance enough ; and so forth.

VIII. *Popular.*

(1) It is a wild idea put forth by a set of cranks, who would be better occupied in something else.

(2) It is impossible.

(3) It is too hard : life isn't long enough.

(4) It is not hard enough : lessons will be too quickly done, and will not sink into the mind.

(5) It will oust all other languages, and thus destroy each nation's birthright and heritage.

(6) It will not come in in our time, so the question is of no interest except to our grandchildren.

(7) It is doomed to failure—look at Volapük!

(8) There are quite enough languages already.

(9) You have to learn three or four languages in order to understand Esperanto.

(10) You cannot know it without learning it.

(11) You have to wear a green star.

Pains have been taken to make this list exhaustive. If any reader can think of another objection, he is requested to communicate with the author.

Most of the serious arguments have been already dealt with, so that not many words need be said here. As regards No. VII. (Technical), this is not the place to deal with actual criticisms of the language (Esperanto) that holds the field. The reader will not be in a position to judge of them till he has learnt it. Suffice it to say that they can all be met, and some of the points criticised as vices are, in reality, virtues in an artificial language.

As for Nos. II. and IV. (Sentimental and Literary), most of these objections are due to the old heresy of the literary man, that an artificial language claims to compete with natural languages *as a language.* Once realize that it is primarily a labour-saving device, and therefore to be judged like any other modern invention such as telegraphy or shorthand, and most of these objections fall to the ground.

A good many of the objections cannot be taken seriously (though they have all been seriously made), or refute themselves or each other. No. VIII. (10) sounds like a fake, but this was the criticism of a scholar and linguist who had been persuaded to look at Esperanto. He complained that though he, knowing Latin, French, Italian, German, and English, could read it without ever having learnt it, ordinary Englishmen could not. It is usual to judge an invention by efficiency compared to cost, but if an appliance is to be condemned because it needs some trouble to master it, then not many inventions will survive.

No. VIII. (9) is of course a mistake. It is like saying that you must practice looping the loop or circus-riding in order to keep your balance on a bicycle. The greater, of course, includes the less; but it is better in both cases to begin with the less. It is much more reasonable to reverse the argument and say : If you begin by learning Esperanto, you will possess a valuable aid towards learning three or four national languages.

No. VIII. (5) is absurd. It is the hardest thing in the world to extirpate a national language ; and all the forces of organized repression (e.g. in unhappy Poland) are finding the task too much for them. What inducement have the common people, who form the bulk of the population in every land, to substitute in their home intercourse for their own language one that they have to learn, if at all, artificially at school ? Only those who have much international intercourse will ever become really at home in international language—i.e. sufficiently at home to make it possible to use it indifferently as a substitute for their mother-tongue ; and people who engage in prolonged and continuous international intercourse, though numerous, will always be in a minority.

XVI

THE WIDER COSMOPOLITANISM—THE COMING OF ASIA

In the civilized West, where pleasure, business, and science are daily forging new ties of common interests between the nations, those engaged in such pursuits have clearly much to gain from the simplification of their pursuits by a common language. But let us look ahead a little further still. It may well be that the outstanding feature of the twentieth century in history will be the coming into line of the peoples of Asia with their pioneer brethren of the West. Look where you will, everywhere the symptoms are plain for those who can read them. Japan has led the way. China is following, and will not be far behind ; eventually, as the Japanese themselves foresee, she will probably outstrip Japan, if

not the world.   There seems to be no ground, ethnological or
otherwise, for thinking that the lagging behind of Asia in modern
civilization corresponds to a real inferiority of powers, mental or
physical, in the individual Asiatic.   Experience shows that under
suitable conditions the Asiatic can efficiently handle all the white
man's tools and weapons ; the complete coming up to date is
largely a matter of organization, education, and the possession of
a few really able men at the head of affairs.   Given these,
progress may be astonishingly quick.   Europeans do not yet seem
to have grasped at all adequately the real significance of the last
fifty years of Japanese history.   Do they really think that the
Chinaman is inferior to the Japanese ?   If so, let them ask any
residents in the Far East.   Can it be maintained that a generation
ago the peasant of Eastern Europe was ahead of the country
Chinaman ?   But the last few years have shown how swiftly
modern civilization spreads, both in Europe and America, from
the comparatively small group of nations which in the main have
worked it out to the others, till lately considered backward and
semi-barbarous.   And this is the case not merely with the material
products of civilization, the railway and the telegraph, but also as
regards its divers manifestations in all that concerns the life of the
people—constitutional government with growth of representative,
elected authorities and democracy ; universal education with
universal power of reading and consequent birth of a cheap press ;
rise of industry and consequent growth of towns ; universal
military service and discipline, now in force in most lands ; rise of
a moneyed and leisured class and consequent growth of sport,
and of all kinds of clubs and societies for promoting various
interests, social, sporting, political, religious, educational, philan-
thropic, and so forth.   In fact, the more the material side of life
is "modernized," the more closely do the citizens of all lands
approximate to one another in their interests and activities, which
ultimately rest upon and grow out of their material conditions.
Meantime wealth and consequently foreign travel everywhere
increase, fresh facilities of communication are constantly pro-

vided, men from different countries are more and more thrown together, and all this makes for the further strengthening of mutual interests and the growth of fresh ones in common.

Now if (1) under the stress of "modernization" life is already becoming so similar in the lands of the West, and if (2) the Asiatic is not fundamentally inferior in mental and physical endowments, then it follows as a certainty that the Asiatic world will, under the same stress, enter the comity of nations, and approximate to the world-type of interest and activity. It is only a question of time. In economic history nothing is more certain than that science, organization, cheapness, and efficiency must ultimately prevail over sporadic, unorganized local effort based on tradition and not on scientific exploitation of natural advantages. Thus the East will adopt the material civilization of the West; and through the same organization of industrial and commercial life and generally similar economic conditions, the same type of moneyed class will grow up, with the same range of interests on the intellectual and social side, diverse indeed, but in their very diversity conforming more and more to the world-type.

Concurrently with this new tendency to uniformity proceeds the weakening of the two most powerful disintegrating influences of primitive humanity—religion and tradition. In the earlier stages of society these are the two most powerful agents for binding together into groups men already associated by the ties of locality and common ancestry, and fettering them in the cast-iron bonds of custom and ceremonial observance. While the members of each group are thus held together by the ideas which appeal most profoundly to unsophisticated mankind, the various groups are automatically and by the same process held apart by the full force of those ideas. Thus are produced castes, with their deadening opposition to all progress; and thus arise crusades, wars of religion and persecutions. Religion and tradition are then at once the mightiest integrants within each single community, and the mightiest disintegrants as between different communities.

But this narrow and dissevering spirit of caste dies back before the spread of knowledge. The tendency to regard a man as unclean or a barbarian, simply because he does not believe or behave as one's own people, is merely a product of isolation and ignorance, and disappears with education and the general opening up of a country. The inquisitor can no longer boast of "strained relations"—strained physically on the rack, owing to differences of religious opinion. The state of things which made it possible for sepoys to revolt because rifle bullets were greased with the fat of a sacred animal, or for yellow men to tear up railway tracks because the magic desecrated the tombs of their ancestors, is rapidly passing away, as Orientals realize the profits to be made from scientific methods.

Thus the levelling influence is at work, and the checks upon it are diminishing. The end can be but one. There will be a greater and greater similarity of life and occupation the world over, and more and more actual and potential international intercourse.

Now, the further we move in this direction, the greater will be the impatience of vexatious restraints upon the freedom of inter-course; and of these restraints the difference of language is one of the most vexatious, because it is one of the easiest to remove. If we devote millions of pounds to annihilating the barriers of space, can we not devote a few months to the comparatively modest effort necessary to annihilate the barriers of language?

A real cosmopolitanism, in the etymological sense of the word, *world* (and not merely European) citizenship, will shift the *onus probandi* from the supporters of an international language to its opponents. It will say to them, "It is admitted that you have much intercourse with other peoples; it is admitted that diversity of language is an obstacle in this intercouse; this obstacle is increasing rather than diminishing as fresh subjects raise their claims upon the few years of education, and the old leisurely type of linguistic education fails more and more to train the bulk of the people for life's business, and as the ranks of the civilized are swelled by fresh peoples for whom it is harder and harder to learn even one Indo-Germanic tongue, let alone several ; it is proved that this obstacle can be removed at the cost of a few months' study : this study is not only the most directly remunerative study in the world, comparing results with cost, but it is an admirable mental discipline and a direct help towards further real linguistic culture-giving studies for those who are fit to undertake them. Show cause, then, why you prefer to suffer under an unnecessary obstacle, rather than avail yourselves of this means of removing it."

It is easier for the Indo-Germanic peoples to learn each other's languages—e.g. for an Englishman to learn Swedish or Russian— than it is for a speaker of one of any of the other families of languages to learn any Indo-Germanic tongue ; so that some idea may be formed of the magnitude of the task imposed upon the newer converts to Western civilization by the Indo-Germanic world, in making them learn one or more of its national languages. At the same time, it is but just that the peoples who have paid the piper of progress should call the common lingual tune. Therefore, what more fitting than that they should provide an essence of their allied languages, reduced to its simplest and clearest form ? This they would offer to the rest of the world to be taken over as part of the general progress in civilization which it has to adopt; and this it is which is provided in the international language, Esperanto.

XVII

IMPORTANCE OF AN INTERNATIONAL LANGUAGE FOR THE BLIND

Now that higher education for the blind is being extended in every country, owing to the more humanitarian feeling of the present age that these afflicted members of the community ought to be given a fair chance, the problem of supplying them with books is beginning to be felt. The process of producing books for the blind on the Braille system is, of course, far more costly than ordinary printing, and at the same time the editions must be necessarily more or less limited. Many an educated blind person is therefore cruelly circumscribed in the range of literature open to him by the mere physical obstacle of the lack of books. This difficulty is accentuated by the fact that three kinds of Braille type are in use—French, English, and American.

Now, suppose it is desired to make the works of some good author accessible to the blind—we will say the works of Milton. A separate edition has to be done into Braille for the English, another separate translation for the French, and so on for the blind of each country. In many cases where translations of a work do not already exist, as in the case of a modern author, the mere cost of translation into some one language may not pay, much less then the preparation of a special Braille edition for the limited blind public of that country. But if one Braille edition is prepared for the blind of the world in the universal auxiliary language, a far greater range of literature is at once brought within their grasp.

Already there is abundant evidence of the keen appreciation of Esperanto on the part of the blind, and one striking proof is the fact that the distinguished French scientist and doctor, Dr. Javal, who himself became blind during the latter part of his life, was, until his death in March 1907, one of the foremost partisans and benefactors of Esperanto. By his liberality much has been rendered possible that could not otherwise have been accomplished. There are many other devoted workers in the same field, among them Prof. Cart and Mme. Fauvart-Bastoul in France, and Mr. Rhodes, of Keighley, and Mr. Adams, of Hastings, in England. A special fund is being raised to enable blind Esperantists from various countries to attend the Congress at Cambridge in August 1907, and the cause is one well worthy of assistance by all who are interested in the welfare of the blind. The day when a universal language is practically recognised will be one of the greatest in their annals.

A perfectly phonetic language, as is Esperanto, is peculiarly suited to the needs of the blind. Its long, full vowels, slow, harmonious intonation, few and simple sounds, and regular construction make it very easy to learn through the ear, and to reproduce on any phonetic system of notation ; and as a matter of fact, blind people are found to enjoy it much. For a blind man to come to an international congress and be able to compare notes with his fellow-blind from all over the world must be a lifting of the veil between him and the outer world, coming next to receiving his sight. To witness this spectacle alone might almost convince a waverer as to the utility of the common language.

XVIII

IDEAL *v.* PRACTICAL

FROM the early days of the Esperanto movement there has flowed within it a sort of double current. There is the warm and genial Gulf Stream of Idealism, that raises the temperature on every shore to which it sets, and calls forth a luxuriant growth of friendly sentiment. This tends to the enriching of life. There is also the cooler current of practicality, with a steady drive towards material profit. At present the tide is flowing free, and, taken at the flood, may lead on to fortune ; the two currents pursue their way harmoniously within it, without clashing, and sometimes mingling their waters to their mutual benefit.

But as the movement is sometimes dismissed contemptuously as a pacifist fad or an unattainable ideal of universal brotherhood, it is as well to set the matter in its true light. It is true that the inventor of Esperanto, Dr. Zamenhof, of Warsaw, is an idealist in the best sense of the word, and that his language was directly inspired by his ardent wish to remove one cause of misunderstanding in his distracted country. He has persistently refused to make any profit out of it, and declined to accept a sum which some enthusiasts collected as a testimonial to his disinterested work.

It is equally true that Esperanto seems to possess a rather strange power of evoking enthusiasm. Meetings of Esperantists are invariably characterized by great cordiality and good-fellowship, and at the international congresses so far these feelings have at times risen to fever heat. It is easy to make fun of this by saying that the conjunction of Sirius, the fever-shedding constellation of the ancients, with the green star * in the dog days of August, when the congresses are held, induces hot fits. Those who have drunk enthusiastic toasts in common, and have rubbed shoulders and compared notes with various foreigners, and gone home having made perhaps lifelong interesting friendships which bring them in touch with other lands, will not undervalue the brotherhood aspect of the common language.

On the other hand, the united Esperantists at their first international meeting expressly and formally dissociated their project from any connection with political, sentimental, or peace-making schemes. They did this by drawing up and promulgating a " Deklaracio," adopted by the Esperantist world, wherein it is declared that Esperanto is a language, and a language only.† It is not a league or a society or agency for promoting any object whatsoever other than its own dissemination as a means of communication. Like other tongues, Esperanto may be used for any purpose whatsoever, and it is declared that a man is equally an Esperantist whether he uses the language to save life or to kill, to further his own selfish ends or to labour in any altruistic cause. ‡

* Badge of the Esperantists.

† For text of this Declaration, see Part II., chap. vii., p. 115.

‡ The non-sectarian nature of Esperanto is shown by the fact that the first two services in the language were held on the same day in Geneva according to the Roman Catholic and Protestant rites. The latter was conducted by an English clergyman, whose striking sermon on unity, in spite of diversity, evidently impressed his international congregation. The Vatican has officially expressed its favour towards Esperanto, and the Archbishop of Canterbury has sanctioned an Esperanto form of the Anglican service, which will be used in London and Cambridge this summer. Cordial goodwill was expressed

The practical nature of the scheme which Esperantists are labouring to induce the world to adopt is thus sufficiently clearly defined. Dr. Zamenhof himself, speaking at the Geneva Congress with all the vivid poignancy attaching to the words of a man fresh from the butcheries at that moment rife in the Russian Empire,* declared that neither he nor other Esperantists were *naïfs* enough to believe that the adoption of their language would put an end to such scenes. But he had *seen* men at each other's throats, beating each other's brains out with bludgeons—men who had no personal enmity and had never seen each other before, but were let loose on each other by pure race prejudice. He *did* claim that mutual incomprehensibility amongst men who thus dwell side by side and should be taking part in a common civic life was one powerful influence in keeping up cliques and divisions, and artificially holding asunder those whom common interests should be joining together. It is hard to refuse credence to this power of language, thus moderately stated.

XIX

LITERARY *v.* COMMERCIAL

ANOTHER vexed question is whether it is advisable to run an international language on a literary or a commercial ticket. On this rock Volapük split—

> A brave vessel,
> That had no doubt some noble creature in her,
> Dashed all to pieces; †

and there was no Prospero to conjure away the tempest and

towards the Vatican, on receipt of its message at Geneva, by speakers who avowed themselves agnostics, but welcomed any advance towards abolition of barriers.

* There were bad massacres about that time in Warsaw, where Dr. Zamenhof lives. During the Congress news came of the assassination of one of the chief civic officials of Warsaw.

† Shakespeare, *The Tempest*.

send everybody safe home to port to speak Volapük happily ever afterwards. The moral is, that it is no good to make exaggerated claims for a universal language. To attempt to set it on a fully equal footing with national languages as a literary medium is to court disaster.

The truth seems to be about this. As a potential means of international communication, Esperanto is unsurpassed, and a long way ahead of any national language. As a literary language, it is far better than Chinook or Pidgin, far worse than English or Greek.

A language, no more than a man, can serve two masters. By attempting to combine within itself this double function an international language would cease to attain either object. The reason is simple.

Its legitimate and proper sphere demands of it as the first essential that it should be easy and universally accessible. This means that the words are to be few, and must have but one clearly marked sense each. There are to be no idioms or set phrases, no words that depend upon their context or upon allusion for their full sense.

On the other hand, among the essentials of a literary language are the exact opposites of all these characteristics. The vocabulary must be full and plenteous, and there should be a rich variety of synonyms ; there should be delicate half-tones and *nuances* ; the words should be not mere counters or symbols of fixed value, determinable in each case by a rapid use of the dictionary alone, but must have an atmosphere, a something dependent upon history, usage, and allusion, by virtue of which the whole phrase, in the finer styles of writing, amounts to more than the sum of the individual meanings of the words which it contains, becoming a separate entity with an individual flavour of its own. To attempt to create this atmosphere in an artificial language is not only futile, but would introduce just the difficulties, redundancies, and complications which it is its chief object to avoid. Take a single instance, Macbeth's—

> Nay, this my hand would rather
> The multitudinous seas incarnadine,
> Making the green one red.

Here the effect is produced by the contrast between the stately march of the long Latin words of thundrous sound, and the short, sharp English. A labour-saving language has no business with such words as "incarnadine" or "multitudinous." In translating such a passage it will reproduce the sense faithfully and clearly, if necessary by the combination of simple roots; but the bouquet of the original will vanish in the process. This is inevitable, and it is even so far an advantage that it removes all ground from the argument that a universal language will kill scholarly language-learning. It will be just as necessary as ever to read works of fine literature in the original, in order to enjoy their full savour; and the translation into the common tongue will not prejudice such reading of originals more than, or indeed so much as, translations into various mother-tongues.

Again, take the whole question of the imitative use of language. In national literatures many a passage, poetry or prose, is heightened in effect by assonance, alliteration, a certain movement or rhythm of phrase. Subtle suggestion slides in sound through the ear and falls with mellowing cadence into the heart. Soothed senses murmur their own music to the mind; the lullaby lilt of the lay swells full the linkéd sweetness of the song.

The How plays fostering round the What. Down the liquid stream of lingual melody the dirge drifts dying—dying it echoes back into a ghostly after-life, as the yet throbbing sense wakes the drowsed mind once more. The Swan-song floats double—song and shadow; and in the blend—half sensuous, half of thought—man's nature tastes fruition.

Now, this verbal artistry, whereby the words set themselves in tune to the thoughts, postulates a varied vocabulary, a rich storehouse wherein a man may linger and choose among the gems of sound and sense till he find the fitting stone and fashion it to one of those—

> jewels five-words long,
> That on the stretched forefinger of all Time
> Sparkle for ever.

But the word-store of an international tongue must not be a golden treasury of art, a repository of " bigotry and virtue." On its orderly rows of shelves must be immediately accessible the right word for the right place : no superfluity, no disorder, no circumambient margin for effect. Homocea-like, it "touches the spot," and having deadened the ache of incomprehensibility, has done its task. " No flowers."

Naturally some peoples will feel themselves more cramped in a new artificial language than others. French, incomparably neat and clear within its limits, but possessing the narrowest " margin for effect," is less alien in its genius from Esperanto than is English, with its twofold harmony, its potentiality (too rarely exploited) of Romance clarity, and its double portion of Germanic vigour and feeling. Yet all languages must probably witness the obliteration of some finer native shades in the international tongue.

But we must not go to the opposite extreme, and deny to the universal language all power of rendering serious thought. Just how far it can go, and where its inherent limitations begin, is a matter of individual taste and judgment. There are Esperanto translations—and good ones—of *Hamlet*, *The Tempest*, *Julius Caesar*, the *Aeneid* of Virgil, parts of Molière and Homer, besides a goodly variety of other literature. These translations do succeed in giving a very fair idea of the originals, as any one can test for himself with a little trouble, but, as pointed out, they must come something short in beauty and variety of expression.

There is even a certain style in Esperanto itself in the hands of a good writer, of which the dominant notes are simplicity and directness—two qualities not at all to be despised. Further, the unlimited power of word-building and of forming terse compounds gives the language an individuality of its own. It contains many expressive self-explanatory words whose meaning can only be conveyed by a periphrasis in most languages,* and this causes it to take on the manner and feel of a *living* tongue, and makes it something far more than a mere copy or barren extract of storied speech.

Technically, the fulness of its participial system, rivalled by Greek alone, and the absence of all defective verbs, lend to it a very great flexibility ; and containing, as it does, a variety of specially neat devices borrowed from various tongues, it is in a sense neater than any of them.

One great test of its capacity for literary expression remains to be made. This is an adequate translation of the Bible. A religious society, famed for the variety of its translations of the Scriptures into every conceivable language, when approached on the subject, replied that Esperanto was not a language. But Esperantists will not "let it go at that." Besides Dr. Zamenhof's own *Predikanto* (Ecclesiastes), an experiment has been made by two Germans, who published a translation of St. Matthew's Gospel. It is not a success, and further experiments have just been made by Prof. Macloskie, of Princeton, U.S.A., and by E. Metcalfe, M.A. (Oxon), I cannot say with what result, not having seen copies.†

From one point of view, the directness and simplicity of the Bible would seem to lend themselves to an Esperanto dress ; but there are certain great difficulties, such as technical expressions, archaic diction, and phrases hallowed by association. A meeting of those interested in this great work will take place

---

* e.g. *samideano*=partisan of the same cause or idea.

     vivipova lingvo=language capable of independent vigorous existence.

† Cf. also now the " Ordo de Diservo " (special Anglican Church service), selected and translated from Prayer Book and Bible for use in England by the Rev. J. C. Rust (obtainable from the British Esperanto Association, 13, Arundel Street, Strand, price 7*d.*).

at Cambridge during the Congress (August 1907). Experimenters in this field will there be brought together from all countries, the subject will be thoroughly discussed, and substantial progress may be hoped for.

In the field of rendering scientific literature and current workaday prose, whose matter is of more moment than its form, Esperanto has already won its spurs. Its perfect lucidity makes it particularly suitable for this form of writing.

The conclusion then is, that Esperanto is neither wholly commercial nor yet literary in the full sense 'in which a grown language is literary ; but it does do what it professes to do, and it is all the better for not professing the impossible.

XX

IS AN INTERNATIONAL LANGUAGE A CRANK'S HOBBY ?

THE apostle of a universal language is made to feel pretty plainly that he is regarded as a crank. He may console himself with the usual defence that a crank is that which makes revolutions; but for all that, it is chilling to be met with a certain smile.

Let us analyse that smile. It varies in intensity, ranging from the scathing sneer damnatory to the gentle dimple deprecatory. But in any case it belongs to the category of the smile that won't come off. I know that grin—it comes from Cheshire.

What, then, do we mean when we smile at a crank ? Firstly and generally that we think his ideal impracticable. But it has been shown that an international language is not impracticable. This alone ought to go far towards removing it from the list of cranks' hobbies.

Secondly, we often mean that the ideal in question is opposed to common sense—e.g. when we smile at a man who lives on protein biscuits or walks about without a hat. We do not impugn the feasibility of his diet or apparel, but we think he is going out of his way to be peculiar without reaping adequate advantage by his departure from customary usage.

The test of "crankiness," then, lies in the adequacy of the advantage reaped. A man who learns and uses Esperanto may at present depart as widely from ordinary usage as a patron of Eustace Miles's restaurant or a member of the hatless brigade ; but is it true that the advantage thereby accruing is equally disputable or matter of opinion ? Is it not, on the contrary, fairly certain that the use of an auxiliary language, if universal, would open up for many regions from which exclusion is now felt as a hindrance ?

Take the case of a doctor, scientist, scholar, researcher in any branch of knowledge, who desires to keep abreast of the advance of knowledge in his particular line. He may have to wait for years before a translation of some work he wishes to read is published in a tongue he knows, and in any case all the periodical literature of every nation, except the one or two whose languages he may learn, will be closed to him. The output of learned work is increasing very fast in all civilized countries, and therefore results are recorded in an increasing number of languages in monographs, reports, transactions, and the specialist press. A move is being made in the right direction by the proposal to print the publications of the Brussels International Bibliographical Institute in Esperanto.

Take a few examples of the hampering effect upon scholarly work of the language difficulty as it already exists. The diffusion of learning will, ironically enough, increase the difficulty.* The late Prof. Todhunter, of Cambridge, was driven to learning Russian for mathematical purposes. He managed to learn enough to enable him to read mathematical treatises ; but how many mathematicians or scientists (or classical scholars, for that matter) could do as much ? And of how much profit was the learning of Russian, *quâ* Russian, to Prof. Todhunter ? It only took up time which could have been better spent, as there cannot be anything very uplifting or cultivating in the language of mathematical Russian.

* By multiplying the languages used.

Prof. Max Müller proposed that all serious scientific work should be published in one of the six languages following— English, French, German, Italian, Spanish, and Latin. But why should other nations have to produce in these languages? and why should serious students have to be prepared to read six languages?

All this was many years ago. The balance of culture has since then been gradually but steadily shifting in favour of other peoples. The present writer had occasion to make a special study of Byron's influence on the Continent. It turned out that one of the biggest and most important works upon the subject was written in Polish. It has therefore remained inaccessible. This is only an illustration of a difficulty that faces many workers.

Thirdly, there is a good large portion of the British public that regards as a crank anything not British or that does not benefit themselves personally. It really *is* hard for an Englishman, Frenchman, or German, brought up among a homogeneous people of old civilization, to realize the extent of the incubus under which the smaller nations of Europe and the polyglot empires further east are groaning. Imagine yourself an educated Swiss, Dutchman, or a member of any of the thirty or forty nationalities that make up the Austrian or Russian Empires. How would you like to have to learn three or four foreign languages for practical purposes before you could hope to take much of a position in life? Can any one assert that the kind of grind required, with its heavy taxation of the memory, is in most cases really educative or confers culture?

Think it out. What do you really mean when you jeer at an Esperantist?

XXI

WHAT AN INTERNATIONAL LANGUAGE IS NOT

An international language is not an attempt to replace or damage in any way any existing language or literature.

XXII

WHAT AN INTERNATIONAL LANGUAGE IS

An international language is an attempt to save the greatest amount of labour and open the widest fields of thought and action to the greatest number.

PART II

HISTORICAL

I

SOME EXISTING INTERNATIONAL LANGUAGES ALREADY IN PARTIAL USE

THOUGH the idea of an artificially constructed language to meet the needs of speakers of various tongues seems for some reason to contain something absurd or repellent to the mind of Western Europeans, there have, as a matter of fact, been various attempts made at different times and places to overcome the obvious difficulty in the obvious way; and all have met with a large measure of success.

The usual method of procedure has been quite rough and ready. Words or forms have been taken from a variety of languages, and simply mixed up together, without any scientific attempt at co-ordination or simplification. The resulting international languages have varied in their degree of artificiality, and in the proportions in which they were consciously or semi-consciously compiled, or else adopted their elements ready-made, without conscious adaptation, from existing tongues. But their production, widespread and continuous use, and great practical utility, showed that they arose in response to a felt want. The wonder is that the world should have grown so old without supplying this want in a more systematic way.

Every one has heard of the *lingua franca* of the Levant. In

74

India the master-language that carries a man through among a hundred different tribes is Hindustanee, or Urdu. At the outset it represented a new need of an imperial race. It had its origin during the latter half of the sixteenth century under Akbar, and was born of the sudden extension of conquest and affairs brought about by the great ruler. Round him gathered a cosmopolitan crowd of courtiers, soldiers, vassal princes, and followers of all kinds, and wider dealings than the ordinary local petty affairs received a great stimulus. Urdu is a good example of a mix-up language, with a pure Aryan framework developed out of a dialect of the old Hindi. In fact, it is to India very much what Esperanto might be to Europe, only it is more empirical, and not so consciously and scientifically worked out.

Somewhat analogous to Urdu, in that it is a literary language used by the educated classes for intercommunication throughout a polygot empire, is the Mandarin Chinese. If China is not "polygot" in the strict technical sense of the term, she is so in fact, since the dialects used in different provinces are mutually incomprehensible for the speakers of them. Mandarin is the official master-language.

Rather of the nature of *patois* are Pidgin-English, Chinook, and Benguela, the language used throughout the tribes of the Congo. Yet business of great importance and involving large sums of money is, or has been, transacted in them, and they are used over a wide area.

Pidgin consists of a medley of words, largely English, but with a considerable admixture from other tongues, combined in the framework of Chinese construction. It is current in ports all over the East, and is by no means confined to China. The principle is that roots, chiefly monosyllabic, are used in their crude form without inflection or agglutination, the mere juxtaposition (without any change of form) showing whether they are verbs, adjectives, etc. This is the Chinese contribution to the language.

Chinook is the key-language to dealings with the huge number of different tribes of American Indians. It contains a large admixture of French words, and was to a great extent artificially put together by the Hudson Bay Company's officials, for the purposes of their business.

Quite apart from these various more or less consciously constructed mixed languages, there is a much larger artificial element in many national languages than is commonly realized. Take modern Hungarian, Greek, or even Italian. Literary Italian, as we know it, is largely an artificial construction for literary purposes, made by Dante and others, on the basis of a vigorous and naturally supple dialect. With modern Greek this is even more strikingly the case. As a national language it is almost purely the work of a few scholars, who in modern times arbitrarily and artificially revived and modified the ancient Greek.

There seems, then, to be absolutely no foundation in experience for opposing a universal language on the score of artificiality.

II

OUTLINE OF THE HISTORY OF THE IDEA OF A UNIVERSAL LANGUAGE

List of Schemes proposed

THE story of Babel in the Old Testament reflects the popular feeling that confusion of tongues is a hindrance and a curse. Similarly in the New Testament the Pentecostal gift of tongues is a direct gift of God. But apparently it was not till about 300 years ago that philosophers began to think seriously about a world-language.

The earliest attempts were based upon the mediaeval idea that man might attain to a perfect knowledge of the universe. The whole sum of things might, it was thought, be brought by division and subdivision within an orderly scheme of classification. To any conceivable idea or thing capable of being represented by human speech might therefore be attached a corresponding word, like a label, on a perfectly regular and logical system. Words would thus be self-explanatory to any person who had grasped the system, and would serve as an index or key to the things they represented. Language thus became a branch of philosophy as the men of the time conceived it, or at all events a useful handmaid. Thus arose the idea of a "philosophical language."

A very simple illustration will serve to show what is meant. Go into a big library and look up any work in the catalogue. You will find a reference number—say, 04582, g. 35, c. If you learnt the system of classification of that library, the reference number would explain to you where to find that particular book out of any number of millions. The fact of the number beginning with a "o" would at once place the book in a certain main division, and so on with the other numbers, till "g" in that series gave you a fairly small subdivision. Within that, "35" gives you the number of the case, and "c" the shelf within the case. The book is soon run to earth.

Just so a word in a philosophical language. Suppose the word is *brabo*. The final *o* shows it to be a noun. The monosyllabic root shows it to be concrete. The initial *b* shows it to be in the animal category. The subsequent letters give subdivisions of the animal kingdom, till the word is narrowed down by its form to membership of one small class of animals. The other members of the class will be denoted by an ordered sequence of words in which only the letter denoting the individual is changed. Thus, if *brabo* means "dog," *braco* may be "cat," and so on : *brado*, *brafo*, *brago* . . . etc., according to the classification set up.

Words, then, are reduced to mere formulae; and grammar, inflections, etc., are similarly laid out on purely logical, systematic lines, without taking any account of existing languages and their structure. To languages of this type the historians of the universal language have given the name of *a priori* languages.

Directly opposed to these is the other group of artificial languages, called *a posteriori*. These are wholly based on the principle of borrowing from existing language: their artificiality consists in choice of words and in regularization and simplification of vocabulary and grammar. They avoid, as far as possible, any elements of arbitrary invention, and confine themselves to adapting and making easier what usage has already sanctioned.

Between the two main types come the *mixed languages*, partaking of the nature of each.

The following list is taken from the *Histoire de la langue universelle*, by MM. Couturat and Leau:

I. A Priori Languages

1. The philosopher Descartes, in a letter of 1629, forecasts a system (realized in our days by Zamenhof) of a regular universal grammar: words to be formed with fixed roots and affixes, and to be in every case immediately decipherable from the dictionary alone. He rejects this scheme as fit "for vulgar minds," and proceeds to sketch the outline of all subsequent "philosophic" languages. Thus the great thinker anticipates both types of universal language.

2. Sir Thomas Urquhart, 1653—*Logopandekteision* (see next chapter).

3. Dalgarno, 1661—*Ars Signorum.*

Dalgarno was a Scotchman born at Aberdeen in 1626. His language is founded on the classification of ideas. Of these there are seventeen main classes, represented by seventeen letters. Each letter is the initial of all the words in its class.

4. Wilkins, 1668—*An Essay towards a Real Character and a Philosophical Language.*

Wilkins was Bishop of Chester, and first secretary and one of the founders of the Royal Society. Present members please note. His system is a development of Dalgarno's.

5. Leibnitz, 1646–1716.

Leibnitz thought over this matter all his life, and there are various passages on it scattered through his works, though no one treatise is devoted to it. He held that the systems of his predecessors were not philosophical enough. He dreamed of a logic of thought applicable to all ideas. All complex ideas are compounds of simple ideas, as non-primary numbers are of primary numbers. Numbers can be compounded *ad infinitum*. So if numbers are translated into pronouncible words, these words can be combined so as to represent every possible idea.

6. Delormel, 1795 (An III)—*Projet d'une langue universelle*.

Delormel was inspired by the humanitarian ideas of the French Revolution. He wished to bring mankind together in fraternity. His system rests on a logical classification of ideas on a decimal basis.

7. Jean François Sudre, 1817—*Langue musicale universelle*.

Sudre was a schoolmaster, born in 1787. His language is founded on the seven notes of the scale, and he calls it Solrésol.

8. Grosselin, 1836—*Système de langue universelle*.

A language composed of 1500 words, called "roots," with 100 suffixes, or modifying terminations.

9. Vidal, 1844—*Langue universelle et analytique*.

A curious combination of letters and numbers.

10. Letellier, 1852–1855—*Cours complet de langue universelle*, and many subsequent publications.

Letellier was a former schoolmaster and school inspector. His system is founded on the "theory of language," which is that the word ought to represent by its component letters an analysis of the idea it conveys.

11. Abbé Bonifacio Sotos Ochando, 1852, Madrid.

The abbé had been a deputy to the Spanish Cortes, Spanish

master to Louis Philippe's children, a university professor, and director of a polytechnic college in Madrid, etc. His language is a logical one, intended for international scientific use, and chiefly for writing. He does not think a spoken language for all purposes possible.

12. *Société internationale de linguistique.* First report dated 1856.

The object of the society was to carry out a radical reform of French orthography, and to prepare the way for a universal language—"the need of which is beginning to be generally felt." In the report the idea of adopting one of the most widely spoken national languages is considered and rejected. The previous projects are reviewed, and that of Sotos Ochando is recommended as the best. The *a posteriori* principle is rejected and the *a priori* deliberately adopted. This is excusable, owing to the fact that most projects hitherto had been *a priori*. The philosopher Charles Renouvier gave proof of remarkable prescience by condemning the *a priori* theory in an article in *La Revue*, 1855, in which he forecasts the *a posteriori* plan.

13. Dyer, 1875—*Lingualumina ; or, the Language of Light.*

14. Reinaux, 1877.

15. Maldent, 1877—*La langue naturelle.*
The author was a civil engineer.

16. Nicolas, 1900—*Spokil.*
The author is a ship's doctor and former partisan of Volapük.

17. Hilbe, 1901—*Die Zahlensprache.*
Based on numbers which are translated by vowels.

18. Dietrich, 1902—*Völkerverkehrssprache.*

19. Mannus Talundberg, 1904—*Perio, eine auf Logik und Gedächtnisskunst aufgebaute Weltsprache.*

II. Mixed Languages

These are chiefly Volapük and its derivates.

1. August Theodor von Grimm, state councillor of the Russian Empire, worked out a "programme for the formation of a universal language," which contains some *a priori* elements, as well as nearly all the principles which subsequent authors of *a posteriori* languages have realized.

This Grimm is not to be confused with the famous philologist Jacob von Grimm, though he wrote about the same time.

2. Schleyer, 1879—*Volapük*.   (See below, p. 92.)

3. Verheggen, 1886—*Nal Bino*.

4. Menet, 1886—*Langue universelle*.
An imitation of Volapük.

5. Bauer, 1886—*Spelin*.
A development of Volapük with more words taken from neutral languages.

6. St. de Max, 1887—*Bopal*.
An imitation of Volapük.

7. Dormoy, 1887—*Balta*.
A simplification of Volapük.

8. Fieweger, 1893—*Dil*.
An exaggeration of Volapük for good and ill.

9. Guardiola, 1893—*Orba*.
A fantastic language.

10. W. von Arnim, 1896—*Veltparl*.
A derivative of Volapük.

11. Marchand, 1898—*Dilpok*.
Simplified Volapük.

6

12. Bollack, 1899—*La langue bleue*.

Aims merely at commercial and common use. Ingenious, but too difficult for the memory.

III. A Posteriori Languages.

1. Faiguet, 1765—*Langue nouvelle*.

Faiguet was treasurer of France. He published his project, which is a scheme for simplifying grammar, in the famous eighteenth-century encyclopaedia of Diderot and d'Alembert.

2. Schipfer, 1839—*Communicationssprache*.

This scheme has an historical interest for two reasons. First, the fact that it is founded on French reflects the feeling of the time that French was, as he says, "already to a certain extent a universal language." The point of interest is to compare the date when the projects began to be founded on English. In 1879 Volapük took English for the base. Secondly, Schipfer's scheme reflects the new consciousness of wider possibilities that were coming into the world with the development of means of communication by rail and steamboat. The author recommends the utility of his project by referring to "the new way of travelling."

3. De Rudelle, 1858—*Pantos-Dimon-Glossa*.

De Rudelle was a modern-language master in France and afterwards at the London Polytechnic. His language is based on ten natural languages, especially Greek, Latin, and the modern derivatives of Latin, with grammatical hints from English, German, and Russian. It is remarkable for having been the first to embody several principles of the first importance, which have since been more fully carried out in other schemes, and are now seen to be indispensable. Among these are: (1) distinction of the parts of speech by a fixed form for each; (2) suppression of separate verbal forms for each person; (3) formation of derivatives by means of suffixes with fixed meanings.

4. Pirro, 1868—*Universalsprache.*

Based upon five languages—French, German, English, Italian, and Spanish—and containing a large proportion of words from the Latin.

5. Ferrari, 1877—*Monoglottica* (?).

6. Volk and Fuchs, 1883—*Weltsprache.*
Founded on Latin.

7. Cesare Meriggi, 1884—*Blaia Zimondal.*

8. Courtonne, 1885—*Langue internationale néo-Latine.*

Based on the modern Romance languages, and therefore not sufficiently international. A peculiarity is that all roots are monosyllabic. The history of this attempt illustrates the weight of inertia against which any such project has to struggle. It was presented to the Scientific Society of Nice, which drew up a report and sent it to all the learned societies of Romance-speaking countries. Answers were received from three towns— Pau, Sens, and Nîmes. It was then proposed to convene an international neo-Latin congress; but it is not surprising to hear that nothing came of it.

9. Steiner, 1885—*Pasilingua.*

A counterblast to Volapük. The author aims at copying the methods of naturally formed international languages like the *lingua franca* or Pidgin-English. Based on English, French, and German; but the English vocabulary forms the groundwork.

10. Eichhorn, 1887—*Weltsprache.*

Based on Latin. A leading principle is that each part of speech ought to be recognizable by its form. Thus nouns have two syllables; adjectives, three; pronouns, one; verbal roots, one syllable beginning and ending with a consonant; and so on.

11. Zamenhof, 1887—*Esperanto.* (See below, p. 105.)

12. Bernhard, 1888—*Lingua franca nuova*.

A kind of bastard Italian.

13. Lauda, 1888—*Kosmos*.

Draws all its vocabulary from Latin.

14. Henderson, 1888—*Lingua*.

Latin vocabulary with modern grammar.

15. Henderson, 1902—*Latinesce*.

A simpler and more practical adaptation of Latin by the same author—*e.g.* the present infinitive form does duty for several finite tenses, and words are used in their modern senses.

16. Hoinix (pseudonym for the same indefatigable Mr. Henderson), 1889—*Anglo-franca*.

A mixture of French and English. Both this and the barbarized Latin schemes are fairly easy and certainly simpler than the real languages, but they are shocking to the ear, and produce the effect of mutilation of language.

17. Stempel, 1889—*Myrana*.

Based on Latin with admixture of other languages.

18. Stempel, 1894—*Communia*.

A simplification of No. 17, with a new name.

19. Rosa, 1890—*Nov Latin*.

A set of rules for using the Latin dictionary in a certain way as a key to produce something that can be similarly deciphered.

20. Julius Lott, 1890—*Mundolingue*.

Founded on Latin. Lott started an international society for a universal language, proposing to build up his language by collaboration of savants thus brought together.

21. Marini, 1891—*Méthode rapide, facile et certaine pour construire un idiome universel*.

22. Liptay, 1892—*Langue catholique*.

Based on the theory than an international language already exists (in the words common to many languages), and has only to be discovered.

23. Mill, 1893—*Anti-Volapük*.

A simple universal grammar to be applied to the vocabulary of each national language.

24. Braakman, 1894—*Der Wereldtaal "El Mundolinco," Gramatico del Mundolinco pro li de Hollando Factore* (Noordwijk).

25. Albert Hoessrich (date ?)—*Talnovos, Monatsschrift für die Einführung und Verbreitung der allgemeinen Verkehrssprache "Tal"* (Sonneberg, Thuringen).

26. Heintzeler, 1895—*Universala*.

Heintzeler compares the twelve chief artificial languages already proposed, and shows that they have much in common. He suggests a commission to work out a system on an eclectic basis.

27. Beermann, 1895—*Novilatin*.

Latin brought up to date by comparison with six chief modern languages.

28. *Le Linguist*, 1896-7.

A monthly review conducted by a band of philologists. It contains many discussions of the principles which should underly an international language, and suggestions, but no complete scheme.

29. Puchner, 1897—*Nuove Roman*.

Based largely on Spanish, which the author considers the best of the Romance tongues.

30. Nilson—*La vest-europish central-dialekt* (1890); *Lasonebr, un transitional lingvo* (1897); *Il dialekt Centralia, un compromiss*

entr il lingu universal de Akademi international e la vest-europish central-dialekt (1899).

31. Kürschner, 1900—*Lingua Komun.*

The author was an Esperantist, but found Esperanto not scientific enough. It is almost incredible that a man who knew Esperanto should invent a language with several conjugations of the verb, but this is what Kürschner has done.

32. International Academy of Universal Language, 1902—*Idiom Neutral.* (See below, p. 98.)

33. Elias Molee, 1902—*Tutonish; or, Anglo-German Union Tongue. Tutonish: a Teutonic International Language* (1904).

34. Molenaar—*Panroman, skiz de un ling internazional* (in *Die Religion der Menschheit,* March 1903); *Esperanto oder Panroman? Das Weltsprache-problem und seine einfachste Lösung* (1906); *Universal Ling-Panroman* (in *Menschheitsziele,* 1906); *Gramatik de Universal* (Leipzig, Puttmann, 1906).

35. Peano—*De Latino sine flexione* (in *Revue de Mathématique,* vol. viii., Turin, 1903); *Il Latino quale lingua ausiliare internazionale* (in *Atti della R. Accademia delle Scienze di Torino,* 1904); *Vocabulario de Latino internationale comparato cum Anglo, Franco, Germano, Hispano, Italo, Russo, Graeco, et Sanscrito* (Turin, 1904). See also the *Formulario mathematico,* vol. v. (Turin, 1906).

36. Hummler, 1904—*Mundelingua* (Saulgau).

37. Victor Hely, 1905—*Esquisse d'une grammaire de la langue internationale,* 1st part: *Les mots et la syntaxe* (Langres).

38. Max Wald, 1906—*Pankel* (*Weltsprache*), *die leichteste und kürzeste Sprache für den internationalen Verkehr. Grammatik und Wörterbuch mit Aufgabe der Wortquelle* (Gross-Beeren).

39. Greenwood, 1906—*Ekselsiore, the New Universal Language for All Nations: a Simplified, Improved Esperanto* (London, Miller & Gill); *Ulla, t ulo lingua ä otrs* (The Ulla Society, Bridlington, 1906).

40. Trischen, 1907—*Mondlingvo, provisorische Aufstellung einer internationalen Verkehrssprache* (Pierson, Dresden).

III

THE EARLIEST BRITISH ATTEMPT

A PERUSAL of the foregoing list shows that in the early days of the search for an international language the British were well to the fore. Of the British pioneers in this field the first two were Scots—a fact which accords well with the traditional enterprise north of the Tweed, and readiness to look abroad, beyond their own noses, or, in this case, beyond their own tongues. It is likewise remarkable that the British have almost dropped out of the running in recent times, as far as origination is concerned. Is this fact also typical, a small symptom of Jeshurun's general fatness? Does it reflect a lesser degree of nimbleness in moving with the spirit of the times?

Anyhow, in this case the Briton's content with what he has got at home is well grounded. He certainly possesses a first-class language. As a curious example of the quaint use of it by a scholar and clever man in the middle of the seventeenth century, the following account of Sir Thomas Urquhart's book may be of some interest.

Sir Thomas is well known as the translator of Rabelais; and evidently something of the curious erudition, polyglotism, and quaintness of conceit of his author stuck to the translator. This book is the rarest of his tracts, all of which are uncommon, and has been hardly more than mentioned by name by the previous writers on the subject.

The title-page runs:

LOGOPANDEKTEISION

Or, An Introduction to the Universal Language, digested into these Six Several Books

Neaudethaumata	Chryseomystes
Chrestasebeia	Neleodicastes
Cleronomaporia	Philoponauxesis

By Sir Thomas Urquhart, of Cromartie, Knight,

Now lately contrived and published both for his own Utilitie, and that of all Pregnant and Ingenious Spirits.

LONDON

Printed and are to be sold by Giles Calvert at the Black Spread-Eagle at the West-end of Paul's, and by Richard Tomlins at the Sun and Bible near Pye Corner. 1653.

In a note at the end of the book he apologizes for haste, saying that the copy was "given out to two several printers, one alone not being fully able to hold his quill a-going."

The book opens with :

"The Epistle Dedicatory to Nobody."

The first paragraph runs :

"Most Honourable,

"My non-supponent Lord, and Soveraign Master of contradictions in adjected terms, that unto you I have presumed to tender the dedicacie of this introduction, will not seem strange to those, that know how your concurrence did further me to the accomplishment of that new Language, into the frontispiece whereof it is permitted."

After some preliminary remarks, he says :

"Now to the end the Reader may be more enamoured of the Language, wherein I am to publish a grammar and lexicon,

I will here set down some few qualities and advantages peculiar to itself, and which no Language else (although all other concurred with it) is able to reach unto."

There follow sixty-six "qualities and advantages," which contain the only definite information about the language, for the promised grammar and lexicon never appeared. A few may be quoted as typical of the inducements held out to "pregnant and ingenious spirits," to the end they "may be more enamoured of the Language." The good Sir Thomas was plainly an optimist.

". . . Sixthly, in the cases of all the declinable parts of speech, it surpasseth all other languages whatsoever : for whilst others have but five or six at most, it hath ten, besides the nominative.

". . . Eighthly, every word capable of number is better provided therewith in this language, then [sic] by any other : for instead of two or three numbers which others have, this affordeth you four; to wit, the singular, dual, plural, and redual.

". . . Tenthly, in this tongue there are eleven genders ; wherein likewise it exceedeth all other languages.

". . . Eleventhly, Verbs, Mongrels, Participles, and Hybrids have all of them ten tenses, besides the present : which number no language else is able to attain to.

". . . Thirteenthly, in lieu of six moods, which other languages have at most, this one enjoyeth seven in its conjugable words."

Sir Thomas evidently believed in giving his clients plenty for their money. He is lavish of "Verbs, Mongrels, Participles, and Hybrids," truly a tempting menagerie. He promises, however, a time-reduction on learning a quantity:

". . . Seven and fiftiethly, the greatest wonder of all is that of all the languages in the world it is easiest to learn; a boy of ten years old being able to attain to the knowledge thereof in three months' space; because there are in it many facilitations for the memory, which no other language hath but itself."

Seventeenth-century boys of tender years must have had a good stomach for "Mongrels and Hybrids," and such-like dainties of the grammatical *menu*; but even if they could swallow a mongrel, it is hard to believe that they would not have strained at ten cases in three months.   It might be called "casual labour," but it would certainly have been "three months' hard."

After these examples of grammatical generosity, it is not sur-prising to read :

"... Fifteenthly, in this language the Verbs and Participles have four voices, although it was never heard that ever any other language had above three."

Note that the former colleagues of the "Verbs and Participles," the "Mongrels and Hybrids," are here dropped out of the category. Perhaps it is as well, seeing the number of voices attributed to each.   A four-voiced mongrel would have gone one better than the triple-headed hell-hound Cerberus, and created quite a special Hades of its own for schoolboys, to say nothing of light sleepers.

Under "five and twentiethly" we learn that "there is no Hexameter, Elegiack, Saphick, Asclepiad, Iambick, or any other kind of Latin or Greek verse, but I will afford you another in this language of the same sort"; which leads up to :

"... Six and twentiethly, as it trotteth easily with metrical feet, so at the end of the career of each line, hath it dexterity, after the manner of our English and other vernaculary tongues, to stop with the closure of a rhyme; in the framing whereof, the well-versed in that language shall have so little labour, that for every word therein he shall be able to furnish at least five hundred several monosyllables of the same termination with it."

A remarkable opportunity for every man to become his own poet !

". . . Four and thirtiethly, in this language also words expressive of herbs represent unto us with what degree of cold, moisture, heat, or dryness they are qualified, together with some other property distinguishing them from other herbs."

In this crops out the idea that haunted the minds of mediaeval speculators on the subject: that language could play a more important part than it had hitherto done; that a word, while conveying an idea, could at the same time in some way describe or symbolize the attributes of the thing named. Imagine the charge of thought that could be rammed into a phrase in such a language. Imagine too, you who remember the cold shudder of your childhood, when you heard the elders discussing a prospective dose—intensified by all the horrors of imagination when the discussion was veiled in the "decent obscurity" of French— imagine the grim realism of a language containing "*words expressive of herbs,*"—and expressive to that extent !

There seems, indeed, to have been something rather cold-blooded about this language :

". . . Eight and thirtiethly, in the contexture of nouns, pronouns, and preposital articles united together, it administreth many wonderful varieties of Laconick expressions, as in the Grammar thereof shall more at large be made known unto you."

But, after all, it had a human side :

". . . Three and fourtiethly, as its interjections are more numerous, so are they more emphatical in their respective expression of passions, than that part of speech is in any other language whatsoever.

". . . Eight and fourtiethly, of all languages this is the most compendious in complement, and consequently fittest for Courtiers and Ladies."

Sir Thomas seems to have been a bit of a man of the world too.

". . . Fiftiethly, no language in matter of Prayer and Ejaculations to Almighty God is able, for conciseness of expression to compare with it ; and therefore, of all other, the most fit for the use of Churchmen and spirits inclined to devotion."

This "therefore," with its direct deduction from "conciseness of expression," recalls the lady patroness who chose her incumbents for being fast over prayers. She said she could always pick out a parson who read service daily by his time for the Sunday service.

Sir Thomas is perhaps over-sanguine to a modern taste when he concludes :

" Besides the sixty and six advantages above all other languages, I might have couched thrice as many more of no less consideration than the aforesaid, but that these same will suffice to sharpen the longing of the generous Reader after the intrinsecal and most researched secrets of the new Grammar and Lexicon which I am to evulge."

IV

HISTORY OF VOLAPÜK—A WARNING

VOLAPÜK is the invention of a " white night." Those who know their *Alice in Wonderland* will perhaps involuntarily conjure up the picture of the kindly and fantastic White Knight, riding about on a horse covered with mousetraps and other strange caparisons, which he introduced to all and sundry with the unfailing remark, " It's my own invention." Scoffers will not be slow to find in Volapük and the White Knight's inventions a common characteristic—their fantasticness. Perhaps there really is some analogy in the fact that both inventors had to mount their hobby-horses and ride errant through sundry lands, thrusting their creations on an unwilling world. But the particular kind of white night of which Volapük was born is the *nuit blanche*, literally = "white night," but idiomatically = "night of insomnia."

On the night of March 31, 1879, the good Roman Catholic Bishop Schleyer, curé of Litzelstetten, near Constance, could not get to sleep. From his over-active brain, charged with a knowledge of more than fifty languages, sprang the world-speech, as Athene sprang fully armed from the brain of Zeus. At any rate, this is the legend of the origin of Volapük.

As for the name, an Englishman will hardly appreciate the fact that the word "Volapük" is derived from the two English words "world" and "speech." This transformation of "world" into *vol* and "speech" into *pük* is a good illustration of the manner in which Volapük is based on English, and suggests at once a criticism of that all-important point in an artificial language, the vocabulary. It is too arbitrary.

Published in 1880, Volapük spread first in South Germany, and then in France, where its chief apostle was M. Kerckhoffs, modern-language master in the principal school of commerce in Paris. He founded a society for its propagation, which soon numbered among its members several well-known men of science and letters. The great Magasins du Printemps—a sort of French Whiteley's, and familiar to all who have shopped in Paris—started a class, attended by over a hundred of its employees; and altogether fourteen different classes were opened in Paris, and the pupils were of a good stamp.

Progress was extraordinarily rapid in other European countries, and by 1889, only nine years after the publication of Volapük, there were 283 Volapük societies, distributed throughout Europe, America, and the British Colonies. Instruction books were published in twenty-five languages, including Volapük itself; numerous newspapers, in and about Volapük, sprang up all over the world; the number of Volapükists was estimated at a million. This extraordinarily rapid success is very striking, and seems to afford proof that there is a widely felt want for an international language. Three Volapük congresses were held, of which the third, held in Paris in 1889, with proceedings entirely in Volapük, was the most important.

The rapid decline of Volapük is even more instructive than its sensational rise. The congress of Paris marked its zenith : hopes ran high, and success seemed assured. Within two years it was practically dead. No more congresses were held, the partisans dwindled away, the local clubs dissolved, the newspapers failed, and the whole movement came to an end. There only remained a new academy founded by Bishop Schleyer, and here and there a group of the faithful.*

The chief reason of this failure was internal dissension. First arose the question of principle : Should Volapük aim at being a literary language, capable of expressing all the finer shades of thought and feeling ? or should it confine itself to being a practical means of business communication ?

Bishop Schleyer claimed for his invention an equal rank among the literary languages of the world. The practical party, headed by M. Kerckhoffs, wished to keep it utilitarian and practical. With the object of increasing its utility, they proposed certain changes in the language ; and thus there arose, in the second place, differences of opinion as to fundamental points of structure, such as the nature and origin of the roots to be adopted. Vital questions were thus reopened, and the whole language was thrown back into the melting-pot.

The first congress was held at Friedrichshafen in August 1884, and was attended almost exclusively by Germans. The second congress, Munich, August 1887, brought together over 200 Volapükists from different countries. A professor of geology from Halle University was elected president, and an International Academy of Volapük was founded.

Then the trouble began. M. Kerckhoffs was unanimously elected director of the academy, and Bishop Schleyer was made

---

* A Volapük journal still appears in Graz, Stiria—*Volapükabled lezenodik*. The editor has just (March 1907) retired, and the veteran Bishop Schleyer, now seventy-five years old, is taking up the editorship again.

grand-master (*cifal*) for life. Questions arose as to the duties of the academy and the respective powers of the inventor of the language and the academicians. M. Kerckhoffs was all along the guiding spirit on the side of the academy. He was in the main supported by the Volapük world, though there seems to have been some tendency, at any rate at first, on the part of the Germans to back the bishop. It is impossible to go into details of the points at issue. Suffice it to say, that eventually the director of the academy carried a resolution giving the inventor three votes to every one of ordinary members in all academy divisions, but refusing him the right of veto, which he claimed. The bishop replied by a threat to depose M. Kerckhoffs from the directorship, which of course he could not make good. The constitution of the academy was only binding inasmuch as it had been drawn up and adopted by the constituent members, and it gave no such powers to the inventor.

So here was a very pretty quarrel as to the ownership of Volapük. The bishop said it belonged to him, as he had invented it: he was its father. The academy said it belonged to the public, who had a right to amend it in the common interest. This child, which had newly opened its eyes and smiled upon the world, and upon which the world was then smiling back—was it a son domiciled in its father's house and fully *in patria potestate*? or a ward in the guardianship of its chief promoters? or an orphan foundling, to be boarded out on the scattered-home system at the public expense, and to be brought up to be useful to the community at large? A vexed question of paternity ; and the worst of it was, there was no international court competent to try the case.

Meantime the congress of 1889 at Paris came on. Volapük was booming everywhere. Left to itself, it flourished like a green bay-tree. This meeting was to set an official seal upon its success ; and governments, convinced by this thing done openly in the *ville lumière*, would accept the *fait accompli* and introduce it into their schools.

Thirteen countries sent representatives, including Turkey and China. The great Kerckhoffs was elected president. The proceedings were in Volapük. The foundling's future was canvassed in terms of himself by a cosmopolitan board of guardians, who did not yet know what he was. Rather a Gilbertian situation. Trying a higher flight, we may say, in Platonic phrase, that Volapük seemed to be about midway between being and not-being. It is a far cry from Gilbert *viâ* Plato to Mr. Kipling, but perhaps Volapük, at this juncture, may be most aptly described as a " sort of a giddy harumphrodite," if not " a devil an' a ostrich an' a orphan-child in one."

Business done : The congress discusses.

The congress passed a resolution that there should be drawn up " a simple normal grammar, from which all useless rules should be excluded," and proceeded to adopt a final constitution for the Volapük Academy.

Article 15 says : " The decisions of the academy must be at once submitted to the inventor. If the inventor has not within thirty days protested against the decisions, they are valid. Decisions not approved by the inventor are referred back to the academy, and are valid if carried by a two-thirds majority."

The bishop held out for his right of absolute veto, as his episcopal fellows and their colleagues are doing " in another place " in England. The conflict presents some analogy with other graver constitutional matters, involving discussion of the respective merits of absolute and suspensive veto, and may therefore have some interest at present, apart from its great importance in any scheme for an international language.

The upshot was that dissensions broke out within the academy. The director, unable to carry a complete scheme of reformed grammar, resigned (1891), and the academy, whose business it was to arrange the next congress and keep the movement going, never convened a fourth congress. Several academicians set to work on new artificial languages of their own ; and what was left of the Academy of Volapük, under a new director, M. Rosenberger, a St. Petersburg railway engineer, elected 1893, subsequently turned its attention to working out a new language, to which was given the name Idiom Neutral (see next chapter).

It is interesting to note that, when Volapük was nearing its high-water mark, the American Philosophical Society appointed a committee (October 1887) to inquire into its scientific value.

This committee reported in November 1887. The report states that the creation of an international language is in conformity with the general tendency of modern civilization, and is not merely desirable, but " *will certainly be realized.*" It goes on to reject Volapük as the solution of the problem, as being on the whole retrogade in tendency. It is too arbitrary in construction, and not international enough in vocabulary ; nor does it correspond to the general trend of development of language, which is away from a synthetic grammar (inflection by means of terminations, as in Latin and Greek) and towards an analytic one (inflection by termination replaced by prepositions and auxiliaries).

But the committee was so fully convinced of the importance of an international language, that it proposed to the Philosophical Society that it should invite all the learned societies of the world to co-operate in the production of a universal language. A resolution embodying this recommendation was adopted by the society, and the invitations were sent out. About twenty societies accepted—among them the University of Edinburgh. The Scots again !

The London Philological Society commissioned Mr. Ellis to investigate the subject, and upon his report declined to co-operate. Mr. Ellis was a believer in Volapük, and furthermore did not agree with the American Philosophical Society's conclusion that an international language ought to be founded on an Indo-Germanic (Aryan) basis. In this Mr. Ellis was almost certainly wrong, as subsequent experience is tending to show. The Japanese, among others, are taking up Esperanto with enthusiasm,

7

find it easy, and make no difficulty about its Aryan basis. But, apart from linguistic considerations, Mr. Ellis's practical reasoning was certainly sound. It was to this effect: The main thing is to adopt a language that is already in wide use and shown to be adequate. Alterations bring dissension; by sticking to what we have already got, imperfections and all, strife is avoided, and the thing is at once reduced to practice.

This was a wise counsel, and applies to-day with double force to the present holder of the field, Esperanto, which is besides, in the opinion of experts, a better language than Volapük, and far easier to acquire.

However, on the question of technical merits, the American Philosophical Society was probably right, as against the London Philological Society represented by Mr. Ellis. And the proof is that Volapük died—primarily, indeed, of dissensions among its partisans, but of dissensions superinduced on inherent defects of principle. That this is true may be seen from the subsequent history of the Volapük movement. This is briefly narrated in the next chapter, under the name of Idiom Neutral.

V

HISTORY OF IDIOM NEUTRAL

WE saw above that M. Kerckhoffs was succeeded in the directorship of the Volapük Academy, 1893, by M. Rosenberger, of St. Petersburg. During his term of office the academy continued its work of amending and improving the language. The method of procedure was as follows: The director elaborated proposals, which he embodied in circulars and sent round from time to time to his fellow-academicians. They voted " Yes " or " No," so that the language, when finished, was approved by them all, and was the joint product of the academy; but it was, in its new form, to a great extent, the work of the director. At the end of his term of office it was practically complete. It had undergone a complete transformation, and was now called Idiom Neutral.

In 1898 M. Rosenberger was succeeded by Rev. A. F. Holmes, of Macedon, New York State. The members of the academy vary from time to time, and include (or have included since 1898) natives of America, Belgium, Denmark, England, France, Germany, Holland, Italy, and Russia.

Dictionaries of Idiom Neutral have been published in English (in America), German, and Dutch ; but the language hardly seems to be in use except among the members of the academy. These do not meet, but carry on their business by means of circulars, drawn up, of course, in Neutral. There are at present only four groups of Neutralists—those of St. Petersburg, Nuremberg, Brussels, and San Antonio, Texas. The famous linguistic club of Nuremberg is remarkable for having gone through the evolution from Volapük to Idiom Neutral *viâ* Esperanto ! Besides these four groups, there are isolated Neutralists in certain towns in Great Britain. The academy seems still to have some points to settle, and the work of propaganda has hardly yet begun.

A paper published in Brussels, under the name of *Idei International*, seems to represent the ideas of scattered Neutralists, and of some partisans of other schemes based on Romance vocabulary. These languages resemble each other greatly, and some sanguine spirits dream that they may be fused together into the ultimate international language. A few even hope for an amalgamation with Esperanto, through the medium of a reformed type of Esperanto, which approximates more nearly to these newer schemes, its vocabulary being, like theirs, almost entirely Romance. A series of modifications was published tentatively by Dr. Zamenhof himself in 1894, but was suppressed from practical considerations, having regard to the fate that overtook Volapük, when once it fell into the hands of reformers. The so-called reforms never represented the real ideas of Zamenhof, and were rather in the nature of reluctant concessions to the weaker brethren. They were never introduced.

The reader may be interested to compare for himself specimens of Volapük, Idiom Neutral (its lineal descendant), and Esperanto. This Esperanto is the only one in use, most Esperantists having never even heard of the reform project, which was at once dropped, before the language had entered upon its present cosmopolitan extension. The following versions of the Lord's Prayer are taken from MM. Couturat and Leau's *History*, as are the facts in the above narratives, with the exception of the latest details :

Volapük

O Fat obas, kel binol in süls, paisaludomöz nem ola ! Kömo-möd monargän ola ! Jenomöz vil olik, äs in sül, i su tal ! Bodi obsik vädeliki givolös obes adelo ! E pardolös obes debis obsik, äs id obs aipardobs debeles obas. E no obis nindukolös in tentadi ; sod aidalivolös obis de bad. Jenosöd !

Idiom Neutral.*

Nostr patr kel es in sieli ! Ke votr nom es sanktifiked ; ke votr regnia veni ; ke votr volu es fasied, kuale in siel, tale et su ter. Dona sidiurne a noi nostr pan omnidiurnik ; e pardona (a) noi nostr debiti, kuale et noi pardon a nostr debtatori ; e no induka noi in tentasion, ma librifika noi da it mal.

Esperanto

Patro nia, kiu estas en la ĉielo, sankta estu via nomo ; venu regeco via ; estu volo via, kiel en la ĉielo, tiel ankaŭ sur la tero. Panon nian ĉiutagan donu al ni hodiaŭ ; kaj pardonu al ni ŝuldojn niajn, kiel ni ankaŭ pardonas al niaj ŝuldantoj ; kaj ne konduku nin en tenton, sed liberigu nin de la malbono.

---

* There are two forms of Idiom Neutral,—one called " pure," authorized by the academy ; the other used in the paper *Idei International.*

Comparing Volapük with Idiom Neutral, even this brief specimen is enough to show the main line of improvement. The framers of the latter had realized the fact that the vocabulary is the first and paramount consideration for an artificial language. It is hopeless to expect people to learn strings of words of arbitrary formation and like nothing they ever saw. Accordingly Idiom Neutral borrows its vocabulary from natural speech, and thereby abandons a regularity which may be theoretically more perfect, but which by arbitrary disfigurement of familiar words overreaches itself, and does more harm than good.

It is very instructive to note that a body of international language specialists were brought little by little to adopt an almost exclusively Romance vocabulary, and this in spite of the fact that they started from Volapük, whose vocabulary is constructed on quite other lines. In other points their language suffers from being too exclusively inspired by Volapükist principles, so that their recognition of the necessity of an *a posteriori* vocabulary is the more convincing.

Given, then, that vocabulary is to be borrowed and not created anew, it is obvious that the principle of borrowing must be *maximum of internationality of roots*—i.e. those words will be adopted by preference which are already common to the greatest number of chief languages. Now, by far the greater number of such international words (which are far more numerous than was thought before a special study was made of the subject) are Romance, being of Latin origin. This is the justification of the prevalence of the Romance element in any modern artificial language. It has been frequently made a reproach against Esperanto that it is a Romance language ; but the unanimous verdict of the competent linguists who composed the academy for the emendation of Volapük may be taken as final. They threshed the question out once for all, and their conclusion derives added force from the fact that it is the result of conversion.

But it may be doubted whether they have not gone rather far in this direction and overshot the mark.

Comparing Idiom Neutral with Esperanto, it will be found that the latter admits a larger proportion of non-Romance words. While fully recognizing and doing justice to the accepted principle of selection, maximum of internationality, Esperanto sometimes gives the preference to a non-Romance word in order to avoid ambiguity and secure a perfectly distinct root from which to form derivatives incapable of confusion with others.*   There is always a good reason for the choice ; but it is easier to appreciate this after learning the language.

But a mere comparison of the brief texts given above will bring out another point in favour of Esperanto—its full vocalic endings. On the other hand, many words in Idiom Neutral present a mutilated appearance to the eye, and, what is a much greater sin in an international language, offer grave difficulties of pronunciation to speakers of many nations.   Words ending with a double consonant are very frequent, e.g. *nostr patr* ; and these will be unpronounceable for many nations, e.g. for an Italian or a Japanese. Euphony is one of the strongest of the many strong points of Esperanto.   In it the principle of maximum of internationality has been applied to *sounds* as well as *forms*, and there are very few sounds that will be a stumbling-block to any considerable number of speakers.   Some of its modern rivals seem to forget that a language is to be spoken as well as written.   When a language is unfamiliar to the listener, he is greatly aided in understanding it if the vowel-sounds are long and full and the pronunciation slow, almost drawling.   Esperanto fulfils these requisites in a marked degree.   It is far easier to dwell upon two-syllabled words with full vocalic endings like *patro nia* than upon awkward words like *nostr patr*.

Yet another advantage of Esperanto is illustrated in the same texts.   Owing to its system of inflexion and the possession of an

---

* It is obvious, too, that English, Germans, and Slavs will be more attracted to a language which borrows some of its features from their own tongues, than to an entirely Romance language.   This relatively wider international appeal is another advantage of Esperanto.

to the common opinion. M. Bollack, author of the *Langue bleue*, has already refused the chairmanship. He does not see the use of founding a fresh academy, and thinks Dr. Molenaar would do better to join forces with the Neutralists.

There exists indeed already an " Akademi International de Lingu Universal," which has produced Idiom Neutral, and of which Mr. Holmes is still director, now in his second term (see preceding chapter). This academy is said to be too one-sided in its composition, and not scientific. But it is hard to see how it will abdicate in favour of a new one.

Meantime, the victorious Esperantists, at present in possession of the field, poke fun at these new-fangled schemes. A parody in Esperanto verse, entitled *Lingvo de Molenaar*, and sung to the tune of the American song *Riding down from Bangor*, narrates the fickleness of Pan-Roman and how it changed into Universal. It is said that a group of Continental Esperantists, at a convivial sitting, burnt the apostate Idiom Neutral in effigy by making a bonfire of Neutral literature. On the other side amenities are not wanting. It is now the fashion to sling mud at a rival language by calling it "arbitrary" and "fantastic"; and these epithets are freely applied to Esperanto. Strong in their cause, the Esperantists are peacefully preparing the Congress of Cambridge.

VII

HISTORY OF ESPERANTO

HAPPY is the nation that has no history,—still happier the international language; for a policy of "pacific penetration" offers few picturesque incidents to furnish forth a readable narrative. In the case of Esperanto there have been no splits or factions; no narrow ring of oligarchs has cornered the language for its own purposes, or insisted upon its aristocratic and non-popular side in the supposed interests of culture or literary taste; consequently there has been no secession of the *plebs*. In the early days of Esperanto there was indeed an attempt to found an Esperanto league; but when it was seen that the league did little beyond suggest alterations, it was wisely dissolved in 1894. Since then Esperanto has been run purely on its merits as a language, and has expressly dissociated itself from any political, pacifist, or other propaganda. Its story is one of quiet progress—at first very slow, but within the last five years wonderfully rapid, and still accelerating. The most sensational episode in this peaceful advance was the prohibition of the principal Esperantist organ by the Russian censorship, so that there is little to do, save record one or two leading facts and dates.

The inventor of Esperanto is a Polish doctor, Ludwig Lazarus Zamenhof, now living in Warsaw. He was born in 1859 at Bielostock, a town which has lately become notorious as the scene of one of the terrible Russian *pogroms*, or interracial butcheries. This tragedy was only the culmination of a chronic state of misunderstanding, which long ago so impressed the young Zamenhof that, when still quite a boy, he resolved to labour for the removal of one cause of it by facilitating mutual intercourse. He has practically devoted his life first to the elaboration of his language, and of later years to the vast amount of business that its extension involves. And it has been a labour of love. Zamenhof is an idealist. His action, in all that concerns Esperanto, has been characterized throughout by a generosity and self-effacement that well correspond to the humanitarian nature of the inspiration that produced it. He has renounced all personal rights in and control of the Esperanto language, and kept studiously in the background till the first International Congress two years ago forced him into the open, when he emerged from his retirement to take his rightful place before the eyes of the peoples whom his invention had brought together.

But he is not merely an idealist: he is a practical idealist. This is shown by his self-restraint and practical wisdom in guiding events. One of the symptoms of "catching Esperanto" is a desire to introduce improvements. This morbid propensity to jejune amateur tinkering, a kind of measles of the mind (*morbus linguificus* *) attacks the immature in years or judgment. A riper acquaintance with the history and practical aims of international language purges it from the system. We have all been through it. For the inventor of Esperanto, accustomed for so many years to retouch, modify, and revise, it must require no ordinary degree of self-control to keep his hands off, and leave the fate of his offspring to others. It grew with his growth, developing with his experience, and he best knows where the shoe pinches and what might yet be done. But he has the fate of Volapük before his eyes. He knows that, having wrought speech for the people, he must leave it to the people, if he wishes them to use and keep using it.

Contrast the uncompromising attitude of the inventor of Volapük, Bishop Schleyer. It will be remembered how he let Volapük run upon the rocks rather than relinquish the helm. He has been nicknamed " the Volapükist Pope "—and indeed he made the great and fatal bull of believing in his own infallibility. Zamenhof has never pretended to this. When he first published his language, he made no claim to finality on its behalf. He called for criticisms, and contemplated completing and modifying his scheme in accordance with them. He even offered to make over this task to a duly constituted academy, if people would come forward and throw themselves into the work. Again, some years later, in a pamphlet, *Choix d'une langue internationale*, he proposed a scheme for obtaining a competent impartial verdict, and declared his willingness to submit to it. At one time he thought of something in the nature of a plebiscite. Later, his renunciation of the last vestige of control, in giving up the *aprobo*, or official sanction of books; his attitude at the international congresses; his refusal to accept the presidency; his reluctance

---

* An expressive (homoeopathic) name for this malady may be coined in Esperanto : *malsano lingvotrudema* = officious or intrusive disease, consisting in an itch for coining language.

to name or influence the selection of the members of the body charged with the control of the language ; his declaration that his own works have no legislative power, but are merely those of an Esperantist ; finally, his sane conception of the scope and method of future development of the language to meet new needs, and of the limits within which it is possible,—all this bespeaks the man who has a clear idea of what he is aiming at, and a shrewd grasp of the conditions necessary to ensure success.

The word Esperanto is the present participle of the verb *esperi* = " to hope," used substantivally. It was under the pseudonym of Dr. Esperanto that Zamenhof published his scheme in 1887 at Warsaw, and the name has stuck to the language. Before publication it had been cast and recast many times in the mind of its author, and it is curious to note that in the course of its evolution he had himself been through the principal stages exhibited in the history of artificial language projects for the last three hundred years. That is to say, he began with the idea of an *a priori* language with made-up words and arbitrary grammar, and gradually advanced to the conception of an *a posteriori* language, borrowing its vocabulary from the roots common to several existing languages and presenting in its grammar a simplification of Indo-European grammar.

He began to learn English at a comparatively advanced stage of his education, and the simplicity of its grammar and syntax was a revelation to him. It had a powerful influence in helping him to frame his grammar, which underwent a new transformation. Specimens of the language as Zamenhof used to speak it with his school and student friends show a wide divergence from its present form. He seems to have had cruel disappointments, and was disillusioned by the falling away of youthful comrades who had promised to fight the battles of the language they practised with enthusiasm at school. During long years of depression work at the language seems to have been almost his one resource. Its absolute simplicity is deceptive as to the immense labour it must have cost a single man to work it out. This is only fully to be appreciated by one who has some knowledge of former attempts. Zamenhof himself admits that, if he had known earlier of the existence of Volapük, he would never have had the courage to continue his task, though he was conscious of the superiority of his own solution. When, after long hesitation, he made up his mind to try his luck and give his language to the world, Volapük was strong, but already involved in internal strife.

Zamenhof's book appeared first in Russian, and the same year (1887) French and German editions appeared at Warsaw. The first instruction book in English appeared in the following year. The only name on the title-page is " St. J.," and it passed quite unnoticed.

Progress was at first very slow. The first Esperanto society was founded in St. Petersburg, 1892, under the name of *La Espero*. As early as 1889 the pioneer Esperanto newspaper, *La Esperantisto*,* conducted chiefly by Russians and circulated mainly in Russia, began to appear in Nüremberg, where there was already a distinguished Volapük club, afterwards converted to Esperanto. Since then Nüremberg has continued to be a centre of light in the movement for an international language. The other pioneer newspapers were *L'Espérantiste*, founded in 1898 at Epernay by the Marquis de Beaufront, and *La Lumo* of Montreal.

In Germany in the early days of Esperanto the great apostles were Einstein and Trompeter, and it was owing to the liberality of the latter that the Nüremberg venture was rendered possible.

Somewhat later began in France the activity of the greatest and most fervent of all the apostles of Esperanto, the Marquis de Beaufront. By an extraordinary coincidence he had ready for the press a grammar and complete dictionary of a language of his own, named *Adjuvanto*. When he became acquainted with Esperanto, he recognized that it was in certain points superior to his own

---

* Afterwards prohibited in Russia, owing to the collaboration of Count Tolstoi, and transferred to Upsala under the name *Lingvo Internacia*. Since 1902 it has been published in Paris.

language, though the two were remarkably similar. He suppressed his own scheme altogether, and threw himself heart and soul into the work of spreading Esperanto. In a series of grammars, commentaries, and dictionaries he expounded the language and made it accessible to numbers who, without his energy and zeal, would never have been interested in it. Among other well-known French leaders are General Sébert, of the French Institute, M. Boirac, Rector of the Dijon University, and M. Gaston Moch, editor of the *Indépendance Belge*.

In England the pioneer was Mr. Joseph Rhodes, who, with Mr. Ellis, founded the first English group at Keighley in November 1902.* Just a year later appeared the first English Esperanto journal, *The Esperantist*, edited by Mr. H. Bolingbroke Mudie, London. Since 1905 it has been incorporated with *The British Esperantist*, the official organ of the British Esperanto Association. The association was founded in October 1904.

The first international congress was held at Boulogne in August 1905. It was organized almost entirely by the president of the local group, M. Michaux, a leading barrister and brilliant lecturer and propagandist. It was an immense success, and inaugurated a series of annual congresses, which are doing great work in disseminating the idea of international language. The second was held in Geneva, August 1906 ; and the third will be held at Cambridge, August 10–17, 1907. It is unnecessary to describe the congresses here, as an account has been given in an early chapter (see pp. 9–12 and 14–15).

Within the last three or four years Esperanto has spread all over the world, and fresh societies and newspapers are springing up on every side. Since the convincing demonstration afforded by the Geneva Congress, Switzerland is beginning to take the movement seriously. Many classes and lectures have been held, and the university is also now lending its aid. In the present

---

* The foundation of the London Esperanto Club took place at practically the same time, and the club became the headquarters of the movement in Great Britain.

year (1907) an International Esperantist Scientific Office has been founded in Geneva, with M. René de Saussure as director, and amongst the members of the auxiliary committee are seventeen professors and eight privat-docents (lecturers) of the Geneva University.

Its object is to secure the recognition of Esperanto for scientific purposes, and to practically facilitate its use. To this end the office carries on the work of collecting technical vocabularies of Esperanto, with the aid of all scientists whose assistance it may receive. This is perhaps the most practical step yet taken towards the standardization of technical terms, which is so badly needed in all branches of science. A universal language offers the best solution of the vexed question, because it starts with a clean sheet. Once a term has been admitted, by the competent committee for a particular branch of science, into the technical Esperanto vocabulary of that science, it becomes universal, because it has no pre-existent rivals ; and its universal recognition in the auxiliary language will react upon writers' usage in their own language.

The Geneva office will also aid in editing scientific Esperantist reviews ; and the chief existing one, the *Internacia Scienca Revuo*, will henceforth be published in Geneva instead of in Paris, as hitherto.

The two principal objects of the Esperantist Scientific Association are :

1. Scientists should always use Esperanto during their international congresses.

2. Scientific periodicals should accept articles written in Esperanto (as they now do in the case of English, French, German, and Italian), and should publish in Esperanto a brief summary of every article written in a national language.

A few weeks after the Geneva Congress there was a controversy on the subject of Esperanto between two of the best known and most widely read Swiss and French newspapers—the Paris *Figaro* and the *Journal de Genève*. The respective champions were

the Comte d'Haussonville, of the Académie Française, and
M. de Saussure, a member of a highly distinguished Swiss
scientific family ; and the matter caused a good deal of interest
on the Continent. France was, in this case, reactionary and
ancien régime : the smaller Republic backed Esperanto and
progress. M. de Saussure brought forward facts, and the count
served up the old arguments about Esperanto being unpatriotic
and the prejudice it would inflict upon literature. The whole
thing was a good illustration of a fact that is already becoming
prominent in the history of the auxiliary language movement—
the scientists are much more favourable than the literary men.
As regards educational reform, the conservative attitude of the
classicists is well known, though there are many exceptions,
especially among real teachers. But it is somewhat remarkable
that, when the proposed reform deals with language, those whose
business it is to know about languages should not take the trouble
to examine the scheme properly, before giving an opinion one
way or the other.

As this question of the attitude of literary men has, and will
have, a vital bearing upon the prospects of international language,
and consequently upon its history, this is perhaps the place
to remove a misunderstanding. A distinguished literary man
objected to the foregoing passage as a stricture upon men of
letters. His point was : " *Of course* literary men care less for
Esperanto than scientific men do : it *must* be so, because they
need it less." Now this is quite true : there is little doubt that
to-day science is, perhaps inevitably, more cosmopolitan than
letters, whatever people may say about " the world-wide republic
of letters." But it does not meet the point. Esperantists do not
complain because men of letters are not interested in Esperanto.
They have their own interests and occupations, and nobody would
be so absurd as to make it a grievance that they will not submit
to have thrust upon them a language for which they have no taste
or use. What Esperantists do very strongly object to is that
some literary men lend the weight of their name and position to

irresponsible criticism.   Let them take or leave Esperanto as
seems good to them.   Their *responsible* opinions, *based upon due
study of the question*, are always eagerly welcomed.   But do not let
them misrepresent Esperanto to the public, thereby unfairly pre-
judicing its judgment.   Such action is unworthy of serious men.
When a man puts forward criticisms of Esperanto based upon
elementary errors of fact, or complains that Esperantists will
not listen to reason because they ignore proposals for change,
which have long ago been threshed out and found wanting, or
are obviously unpractical, he is merely showing that he has not
studied the question.   A fair analogy would be the case of a
chemist or engineer who had recently begun to dabble in Greek
in his spare moments, and who should undertake to emend
the text of Sophocles.   His suggestions would show that he
knew no Greek, that he had never heard of Sir Richard Jebb,
and that he was ignorant of all the results of scientific textual
criticism.   But here comes in the difference.   Such a critic
would be laughed out of court, and told to mind his own
business, or else learn Greek before he undertook to emend
it.   But as international language is a novelty to most people, it
is thought that any one can make, mend, or criticise it.   It is not,
like Greek, yet recognized as a serious subject, and therefore
irresponsible criticism is too apt to be taken at its face value,
merely on the *ipse dixit* of the critic, especially if he happens to
be an influential man in some other line.   Nobody bothers about
his qualifications in international language ; nobody either knows
or cares whether he has any claim to be heard on the subject
at all.

The fact is that international language now has a considerable history behind it.   A large amount of experience has been
amassed, and is now available for any one who is willing and
competent to go into the question.   But, in order to do fruitful
work in this field, it is just as necessary as in any other to be
properly equipped, and to know where others have left off, before
you begin.

At the first international congress at Boulogne the history of Esperanto was well summed up in a thoughtful speech by Dr. Bein, of Poland, himself a considerable Esperantist author, using the *nom de guerre* "Kabe." He pointed out that we are still in the first or propaganda stage of international language, in which it is necessary to hold congresses, and the language is treated as an end in itself. There is good hope that the second stage may soon be reached, in which the language may be sufficiently recognized to take its proper place as a means.

Meantime, the first stage of Esperanto has been marked by three phases or periods—the Russian period, the French period, and the international period. Each has left its mark upon the language.

The Russian period is associated with the names of Kofman, Grabowski, Silesnjov, Gernet, Zinovjev, and many other writers of considerable literary power. Being the pioneers, they had to prove the capabilities of the language to the world, and in doing so they took off some of the rough of the world's indifference and scepticism. The language benefited by the fact that the first authors were Slavs. The simplicity of the Slav syntax, the logical arrangement of the sentences, the perfectly free and natural order of the words, passed unconsciously from their native language to the new one in the hands of these writers, and have been imitated by their successors.

The French period is associated chiefly with the name of M. de Beaufront. In Russia, side by side with the good points named above, certain less desirable Slavisms were creeping in ; also there were hitherto no scientific dictionaries or explanation of syntax. As Dr. Bein says, de Beaufront may be called "the codifier of Esperanto." A goodly band of French writers now took the language in hand, and by their natural power of expression and exposition, which seems inborn in a Frenchman, and by their national passion for lucidity, they have no doubt strengthened the impulse of Esperanto towards clear-cut, vigorous style.

Possibly theorizing has been overdone in France; for, after all, the strong point of Esperanto syntax is that there is none to speak of, common sense being the guide. It is a pity to set up rules where none are necessary, or to do anything that can produce an impression in the minds of the uninitiated that learning Esperanto means anything approaching the memory drudgery necessary in grasping the rules and constructions of national languages.

The third period began soon after the turn of the century, and is still in full force. Take up any chance number of any Esperanto gazette out of the numbers that are published all over the world; you will hardly be able to draw any conclusion as to the nationality of the writer of the article you light upon, save perhaps for an occasional turn of an unpractised hand. Esperanto now has its style; it is—lucidity based upon common sense and the rudiments of a minimized grammar.

This chapter would not be complete without some account of the *constitution* of Esperanto, and the means which have been adopted to safeguard the purity of the language. It will be well to quote in full the Declaration adopted at Boulogne, in which its aim is set forth, and which forms, as it were, its written constitution. For the convenience of readers the Esperanto text and English translation are printed in parallel columns.

DEKLARACIO	DECLARATION
Ĉar pri la esenco de Esperantismo multaj havas tre malveran ideon, tial ni subskribintoj, reprezentantoj de la Esperantismo en diversaj landoj de la mondo, kunvenintaj al la Internacia Kongreso Esperantista en Boulogne - sur - Mer, trovis necesa, laŭ la propono de la	Because many have a very false idea of the nature of Esperanto, therefore we, the undersigned, representing the cause of Esperanto in different countries of the world, having met together at the International Esperanto Congress in Boulogne-sur-Mer, have thought

aŭtoro de la lingvo Esperanto, doni la sekvantan klarigon :

1. La Esperantismo estas penado disvastigi en la tuta mondo la uzadon de lingvo neŭtrale homa, kiu, "ne entrudante sin en la internan vivon de la popoloj kaj neniom celante elpuŝi la ekzistantajn lingvojn naciajn," donus al la homoj de malsamaj nacioj la eblon kompreniĝadi inter si, kiu povus servi kiel paciga lingvo de publikaj institucioj en tiuj landoj kie diversaj nacioj batalas inter si pri la lingvo, kaj en kiu povus esti publikigataj tiuj verkoj kiuj havas egalan intereson por ĉiuj popoloj.

Ĉiu alia ideo aŭ espero kiun tiu aŭ alia Esperantisto ligas kun la Esperantismo estos lia afero pure privata, por kiu la Esperantismo ne respondas.

2. Ĉar en la nuna tempo neniu esploranto en la tuta mondo jam dubas pri tio, ke lingvo internacia povas esti nur lingvo arta, kaj ĉar, el ĉiuj mult-

it necessary, at the suggestion of the author of the Esperanto language, to give the following explanation :

1. Esperanto in its essence is an attempt to diffuse over the whole world a language belonging to mankind without distinction, which, "not intruding upon the internal life of the peoples and in nowise aiming to drive out the existing national languages," should give to men of different nations the possibility of becoming mutually comprehensible, which might serve as a peace-making language for public institutions in those lands where different nations are involved in strife about their language, and in which might be published those works which possess an equal interest for all peoples.

Any other idea or hope which this or that Esperantist associates with Esperanto will be his purely personal business, for which Esperanto is not responsible.

2. Because at the present time no one who looks out over the whole world any longer doubts that an international language can only be an artificial

egaj provoj faritaj en la daŭro de la lastaj du centjaroj, ĉiuj prezentas nur teorajn projektojn, kaj lingvo efektive finita, ĉiuflanke elprovita, perfekte vivipova, kaj en ĉiuj rilatoj pleje taŭga montriĝis nur unu sola lingvo, Esperanto, tial la amikoj de la ideo de lingvo internacia, konsciante ke teoria disputado kondukos al nenio kaj ke la celo povas esti atingita nur per laborado praktika, jam de longe ĉiuj grupiĝis ĉirkaŭ la sola lingvo, Esperanto, kaj laboras por ĝia disvastigado kaj riĉigado de ĝia literaturo.

3. Ĉar la aŭtoro de la lingvo Esperanto tuj en la komenco rifuzis, unu fojon por ĉiam, ĉiujn personajn rajtojn kaj privilegiojn rilate tiun lingvon, tial Esperanto estas "nenies propraĵo," nek en rilato materiala, nek en rilato morala.

Materiala mastro de tiu ĉi lingvo estas la tuta mondo, kaj ĉiu deziranto povas eldonadi en aŭ pri tiu ĉi lingvo ĉiajn verkojn kiajn li deziras, kaj

one, and because, of all the very numerous attempts made in the course of the last two hundred years, all offer merely theoretical solutions, and only one single language, Esperanto, has shown itself to be in practice complete, fully tested on every side, perfectly capable of living use, and in every respect completely adequate, therefore the friends of the idea of international language, recognizing that theoretical discussion will lead to nothing and that the end can only be attained by practical and continuous effort, have long grouped themselves around one single language, Esperanto, and are labouring to disseminate it and to enrich its literature.

3. Because the author of the Esperanto language from the very beginning refused, once for all, all personal rights and privileges connected with that language, therefore Esperanto is "the property of no one," either from a material or moral point of view.

Materially speaking, the whole world is master of this language, and any one who wishes can publish in or about this language works of any kind he wishes,

uzadi la lingvon por ĉiaj eblaj
celoj; kiel spiritaj mastroj de
tiu ĉi lingvo estos ĉiam rigar-
dataj tiuj personoj kiuj de la
mondo Esperantista estos kon-
fesataj kiel la plej bonaj kaj
la plej talentaj verkistoj de tiu
ĉi lingvo.

4. Esperanto havas neniun
personan leĝdonanton kaj de-
pendas de neniu aparta homo.
Ĉiuj opinioj kaj verkoj de la
kreinto de Esperanto havas,
simile al la opinioj kaj verkoj
de ĉiu alia Esperantisto, karak-
teron absolute privatan kaj por
neniu devigan. La sola, unu
fojon por ĉiam deviga por ĉiuj
Esperantistoj, fundamento de
la lingvo Esperanto estas la
verketo *Fundamento de Esperanto*, en kiu neniu havas la
rajton fari ŝanĝon. Se iu de-
kliniĝas de la reguloj kaj mo-
deloj donitaj en la dirita verko,
li neniam povas pravigi sin
per la vortoj "tiel deziras aŭ
konsilas la aŭtoro de Esperanto." Ĉiun ideon, kiu ne
povas esti oportune esprimata
per tiu materialo kiu troviĝas
en la *Fundamento de Esperanto*,
ĉiu havas la rajton esprimi en
tia maniero kiun li trovas la

and go on using the language
for any possible object; from
an intellectual point of view
those persons will always be
regarded as masters of this
language who shall be recognized by the Esperantist world
as the best and most gifted
writers in this language.

4. Esperanto has no personal
law-giver and depends upon no
particular person. All opinions
and works of the creator of
Esperanto have, like the
opinions and works of any
other Esperantist, an absolutely
private character, and are binding upon nobody. The sole
foundation of the Esperanto
language, which is once for all
binding upon all Esperantists,
is the little work *Fundamento
de Esperanto*, in which no one
has the right to make any
change. If any one departs
from the rules and models given
in the said work, he can never
justify himself with the words
"such is the wish or advice of
the author of Esperanto." In
the case of any idea which cannot be conveniently expressed
by means of that material which
is contained in the *Fundamento
de Esperanto*, every Esperantist

plej ĝusta, tiel same kiel estas farate en ĉiu alia lingvo. Sed pro plena unueco de la lingvo, al ĉiuj Esperantistoj estas rekomendate imitadi kiel eble plej multe tiun stilon kiu troviĝas en la verkoj de la kreinto de Esperanto, kiu la plej multe laboris por kaj en Esperanto, kaj la plej bone konas ĝian spiriton.

5. Esperantisto estas nomata ĉiu persono kiu scias kaj uzas la lingvon Esperanto, tute egale por kiaj celoj li ĝin uzas. Apartenado al ia aktiva societo Esperantista por ĉiu Esperantisto estas rekomendinda, sed ne deviga.

has the right to express it in such manner as he considers most fitting, just as is done in the case of every other language. But for the sake of perfect unity in the language, it is recommended to all Esperantists to constantly imitate as far as possible that style which is found in the works of the creator of Esperanto, who laboured the most abundantly for and in Esperanto, and who is best acquainted with the spirit of it.

5. The name of Esperantist is given to every person who knows and uses the Esperanto language, no matter for what ends he uses it. Membership of some active Esperanto society is to be recommended for every Esperantist, but this is not compulsory.

By the wise provision of Article 4, that the entire grammar and framework of Esperanto, as contained within one small book of a few pages, is absolutely unchangeable, the future of the language is secured. The *Fundamento* also contains enough root words to express all ordinary ideas. Henceforth the worst thing that can happen to Esperanto by way of adulteration is that some authors may use too many foreign words. The only practical check upon this, of course, is the penalty of becoming incomprehensible. But as men are on the whole reasonable, and as the only object of writing in Esperanto presumably is to appeal to an Esperantist international public, this check should be sufficient to prevent the use of any word that usage is not tending to consecrate. A certain latitude of expansion must be allowed to every language, to enable it to move with the times ; but beyond this, surely few would have any interest in foisting into their discourse words which their hearers or readers would not be likely to understand, and those few would probably belong to the class who do the same thing in using their mother-tongue. No special legislation is needed to meet their case.

For a few years (1901-1905) the publishing house of Hachette had the monopoly of official Esperanto publications, and no work published elsewhere could find place in the "Kolekto Esperanto aprobita de D°. Zamenhof." But at the first congress Zamenhof announced that he had given up even this control, and Esperanto is now a free language.

The official authority, which deals with all matters relating to the language itself, is the *Lingva Komitato* (Language Committee). It was instituted at the first congress, and consists of persons appointed for their special competence in linguistic matters. The original members numbered ninety-nine, and represented the following twenty-eight countries : Austria, Belgium, Brazil, Bulgaria, Canada, Chili, Denmark, Finland, France, Germany, Great Britain, Greece, Holland, Hungary, Iceland, Italy, Japan, Mexico, Norway, Persia, Peru, Poland, Portugal, Russia, Spain, Sweden, Switzerland, and the United States.

This committee decides upon its own organization and procedure. In practice it selects from among the points submitted to it by Esperantists those worthy of consideration, and propounds them to its members by means of circulars. It then appoints a competent person or small committee to report upon the answers received. Decisions are made upon the result of the voting in the members' replies to the circulars, as analyzed and tabulated in the report. The functions of the committee do not include the making of any alteration whatever in the Esperanto part of the *Fundamento de Esperanto*, which is equally sacrosanct for it and for all Esperantists. But there is much to be done in correcting certain faulty translations of the fundamental Esperanto roots into national languages, in defining their exact meaning and giving their authorized equivalent in fresh languages, into which they were not originally translated.   Also the constantly growing output of grammars and instruction books of all kinds in every country, to say nothing of dictionaries, which are very important, has to be carefully watched, in order that errors may be pointed out and corrected before they have time to take root.

Thus the Lingva Komitato is in no sense an academy or legislative body, having for object to change or improve the language; it is the duly constituted and widely representative authority, which watches the spread and development of the language, maintaining its purity, and helping with judicious guidance.

From this sketch it ought to be clear that Esperanto is no wild-cat scheme of enthusiasts or faddists, but a wisely organized attempt to wipe out the world's linguistic arrears.   Its aim is to bring progress in oral and written communication into line with the progress of material means of communication and of science.

VIII

PRESENT STATE OF ESPERANTO : (*a*) GENERAL ; (*b*) IN ENGLAND

(*a*) General

THE first question usually asked is, " How many Esperantists are there ? "   The answer is, " Nobody knows."   The most diverse estimates have been made, but none are based on any reliable method of computation.   In the *Histoire de la langue universelle*, which appeared in 1903 and is written throughout in an impartial and scientific spirit, 50,000 was tentatively given as a fairly safe estimate.   That was before the days of the international congresses, and since then the cause has been advancing by leaps and bounds. Not a month passes without its crop of new clubs and classes, and the pace is becoming fast and furious.

A marked change has been noticeable of late in the press of the leading countries.   It is becoming a rare thing now to see Esperanto treated as a form of madness, and the days of contemptuous silence are passing away.   Esperanto doings are now fairly, fully, and accurately reported.   The tone of criticism is sometimes favourable, sometimes patronizing, sometimes hostile ; but it is generally serious.   It is coming to be recognized that Esperanto is a force to be reckoned with ; it cannot be laughed off. One or two rivals, indeed, are getting a little noisy.   They are mostly one-man (not to say one-horse) shows, and they do not like to see Esperanto going ahead like steam.   High on the mountainside they sit in cold isolation, and gaze over the rich fertile plains of Esperanto, rapidly becoming populous as the immigrants rush in and stake out their claims in the fair " no-man's land."*   And it makes them feel bad, these others !   " Jeshurun waxed fat," they cry ; " pride goes before a fall, remember Volapük ! "   The Esperantists remember Volapük, close their ranks, and sweep on.

Another good criterion besides the press is the sale of books. Large editions are going off everywhere, especially, it would seem, in America, where the folk have a habit, once they have struck a business proposition, of running it for all it is worth.   " Let her go ! give her hell ! " is the word, and " the boys " are just now getting next to Esperanto to beat the band.

The British Esperanto Association's accounts show a very steady increase in the sale of literature.   Considering that it sells books at trade prices, that hardly any of them are priced at more than a few pence, and none above a shilling or two, the sums realized from sale of books in some months are astonishing, and represent a large and increasing spread of interest among the public.   Owing to the low prices, the profit on books is of course not great ; but, such as it is, it all goes to help the cause. The association is now registered as a non-profit-making society under the law of 1867, with no share capital and no dividends.

As regards official recognition, good progress is being made in

* " *Nenies proprajo*."   Esp. Deklaracio, Art. 3 (see p. 117).

England (see below); but if the language is anywhere adopted universally in government schools, it will certainly be first in France. (For an account of the present state of this question, which is at present before the French Permanent Educational Commission, see Part I., chap. vi., p. 30). Dr. Zamenhof has been decorated by the French Government, and Esperanto is already taught in many French schools. For purposes of education France is divided into districts, called *ressorts d'Académie*, within each of which there is a complete educational ladder from the primary schools to the university which is the culmination of each. The official head of an important district is Rector Boirac, head of the Dijon University. He is one of the most distinguished of the Esperantists, and is the leading spirit at the congresses and on the Lingva Komitato. He has done much for Esperanto in the schools of his district, and under the guidance of men of his calibre Esperanto is making serious progress in France. (For lists of university professors favourable to an international language, see p. 32).

In Germany one of the foremost men of science of his time, Prof. Ostwald, of Leipzig, is an ardent advocate of the international language. He recently was lent for a time to Harvard University, U.S.A., and while there gave a great impetus to the study of Esperanto. He also spoke in its favour at Aberdeen last year, on the occasion of the opening of the new University buildings.

Apropos of the interchange between different countries of professors and other teachers, which has to some extent been already tried between America and Germany, it is curious to note the attitude of Prof. Hermann Diels, Rector of the Berlin University. He is a great supporter of the extension of this interchange, which also has the approbation of the Kaiser, who attended formally the inaugural lecture of one of the American professors, to mark his approbation. Prof. Diels commented on the fact that diversity of language was a grave obstacle; but though he seems before to have been a champion of popularized

Latin, he now declares himself strongly against any artificial language,* and advocates the use of English, French, and German. This is a modified form of the old Max Müller proposal, that all serious scientific work should be published in one of six languages. It does not seem a very convincing attitude to take up, because it ignores the facts: (1) that the actual trend of the world is the other way—towards inclusion of fresh national languages among the *Kultursprachen*, not towards accentuation of the predominance of these three; (2) that the increase of specialization and new studies at universities is leaving less and less time for mastering several difficult languages merely as means to other branches of study. Why should everybody have to learn English, French, and German?

For the rest, Esperanto is now beginning to take hold in Germany. The Germans have, as a general rule, open minds for this kind of problem, and are trained to take objective views in linguistic matters on the scientific merits of the case. The reason why they have been somewhat backward hitherto in the Esperanto movement is no doubt their disappointment at the failure of Volapük, which they had done much to promote. But now that, in spite of this special drawback, the first steps have been made, and clubs and papers are beginning to spring up again, everything points to powerful co-operation from Germany in the future.

In Switzerland progress has been enormous since the Geneva Congress of 1906. Many clubs and classes are already formed or in process of formation, and university men are supporting the movement. In one respect the Swiss are now in the van of the Esperantist world: they have just started a newspaper, *Esperanto*, the prospectus of which declares that it will no longer treat the language as an end in itself, or make propaganda; it will run on the lines of an ordinary weekly, merely using

* Herr Diels quaintly finds that Esperanto has only one gender—the feminine! Surely an ultra-Shavian obsession of femininity. It is perhaps some distinction to out-Shaw Bernard Shaw in any line.

Esperanto as a means, inasmuch as it is the language of the paper.

The well-known Swiss veteran philosopher Ernst Naville wrote to the Geneva Congress that for thirty years he had regarded the introduction of an international language as a necessity, owing to the advance of civilization, and the day of realization of this object would be one of the greatest dates of history.

It is impossible to go through all the countries of Europe in detail. It is probable that the greatest numbers of Esperantists are still to be found among the Slav peoples. The language first took root in their midst, and was spread far and wide by a distinguished group of Slav writers.

Outside Europe, Esperanto is making great strides in the British Empire, Japan, and America. There are now Esperantist clubs in various parts of India, New Zealand, Australia, Canada, in Malta, Singapore, etc. Dr. Pollen, C.I.E., President of the British Esperanto Association, has just been touring in India, in the interests of the language. Among many satisfactory results is the guarantee of handsome sums towards the guarantee fund of the coming Cambridge Congress by several native rulers, among others the Mir of Khairpur, the Raja of Lunawada, the Nawab of Radhanpur, and the Diwan of Palanpur.

In New Zealand, an enterprising pioneer country in many departments, the Prime Minister, Sir Joseph Ward, is favourable. Not long ago he made a speech advocating the introduction of Esperanto into the public schools of the colony.

In America big Esperantist societies and classes have sprung up with amazing rapidity during the last year. Several universities now hold Esperanto classes; the Boston Massachusetts Institute of Technology has more than 100 students in its Esperanto class, and, among schools, the famous Latin School of Roxbury has led the way with over fifty pupils under Prof. Lowell. The press is devoting a large amount of attention to Esperanto, and many journals of good standing are favourable. *The North American Review* has taken up the language. It printed articles in December and January by Dr. Zamenhof and Prof. Macloskie of Princeton, and followed them up by courses of lessons. It supplies Esperanto literature to its readers at cost price, and reports that evidences of interest "have been many and multiply daily."

Among university supporters are Profs. Huntington and Morse of Harvard, Prof. Viles, Ohio State University, Prof. Borgerhoff, Western Reserve University, Prof. Macloskie of Princeton, etc. On the other hand, Prof. Hugo Münsterberg of Harvard is attacking Esperanto. His is a good example of the literary man's uninformed criticism of the universal language project, because it is based upon an old criticism by a German professor (Prof. Hamel) of the defunct Volapük. Why Esperanto should be condemned for the sins of Volapük is not obvious.

One other useful aspect of Esperanto remains to be mentioned —the establishment of consulships to give linguistic and other assistance. Many towns have already their Esperanto consuls, and in a few years there ought to be a haven of refuge for Esperantists abroad nearly everywhere.

The following list of principal Esperanto organs will give some idea of the diffusion of the language. The list makes no pretence of being complete.

Principal general reviews:

Internacia Scienca Revuo.

La Revuo (which enjoys the constant collaboration of Dr. Zamenhof).

Tra la Mondo. (This review has recently held, by the collaboration of its readers, an international inquiry into education in all countries. The report is appearing in the February number and following. This is a good example of the sort of international work which can be done for and by readers in every corner of the globe.)

Other organs:

The British Esperantist.

Lingvo Internacia (the *doyen* of Esperanto journals).

L'Espérantiste (France).

Germana Esperantisto.

Eĥo (Germany).

Svisa Espero.

Esperanto (Switzerland).

Juna Esperantisto (Switzerland).

Esperanto (Hungary).

Helpa Lingvo (Denmark).

La Suno Hispana (Spain).

Idealo (Sicily).

La Alĝera Stelo (Algiers : has recently ceased to appear).

La Belga Sonorilo (Belgium).

Ruslanda Esperantisto (Russia).

Pola Esperantisto (Poland).

Bulgara Esperantisto (Bulgaria).

Lorena Esperantisto.

Esperantisten (Sweden).

Časopis Českych Esperantista (Bohemia).

L'Amerika Esperantisto (central American organ, supported by groups in New York, Chicago, Boston, Philadelphia, Seattle, Los Angeles).

La Lumo (Montreal).

Antaŭen Esperantistoj (Peru).

Brazila Revuo Esperantista (Brazil).

La Japana Esperantisto (Japan).

La Pioniro (India).

Espero Katolika.

Foto Revuo.

Socia Revuo.

Unua Paŝo.

Espero Pacifista.

Eksport Jurnalo.

Esperanta Ligilo (for the blind—in Braille).

The New International Review (Oxford) recently presented a four-page Esperanto supplement to its subscribers for some months.

(b) *Present State of Esperanto in England*

The most practical way of spreading Esperanto is to get it taught in the schools, so it will be best to state first what has been done so far in this matter.

Esperanto has been officially accepted by the local educational authorities in London, Liverpool, Manchester, and other provincial towns ; that is to say, it has been recognized as a subject to be taught in evening classes, if there is sufficient demand. At present there are classes under the London County Council at the following schools : Queen's Road, Dalston (Commercial Centre) ; Blackheath Road (Commercial Centre) ; Plough Road, Clapham Junction (Commercial Centre) ; Rutland Street, Mile End (Commercial Centre) ; Myrdle Street, Commercial Road ; and Hugh Myddleton School, Clerkenwell. Other classes held in London are at the Northern Polytechnic, Holloway Road ; St. Bride's Institute, Bride Lane ; City of London College, White Street ; Co-operative Institute, Plumstead ; Working Men's College, St. Pancras ; Stepney Library, Mile End Road; and a large class for teachers is held at the Cusack Institute, Moorfields.

At Keighley, Yorks, the Board of Education has recognized the language as a grant-earning subject. Various local authorities give facilities, some paying the teacher, others supplying a room. Among these are Kingston-on-Thames (Technical Institute), Rochdale, Ipswich (Technical School), Grimsby, etc.

It does not appear that Esperanto is yet taught in any public elementary school ; educational officials, inspectors, etc., have yet to learn about the language. Many private schools now teach it, and at least one private girls' school of the best type teaches it as a regular subject, alongside French and German. It has been impossible to get any return or figures as to the extent to which it has penetrated into private and proprietary schools. The Northern Institute of Languages, perhaps the most important commercial school in the North of England, held an Esperanto class with sixty-three students.

Two large examining bodies—the London Chamber of Commerce and the Examination Board of the National Union of Teachers—have included Esperanto in their subjects for commercial certificates. At the London Chamber of Commerce examination in May 1906 the candidates were as follows :

	Entries.	Passes.
Teacher's diploma	6	1
Senior	15	15
Junior	109	67
	130	83

There is now a Teachers' Section of the British Esperanto Association with an Education Committee, which is carrying on active work in promoting Esperanto in the schools.

At an official reception of French teachers in London last year by the Board of Education, Mr. Lough, speaking on behalf of the Board, made a sympathetic reference to Esperanto. The incident is amusingly told in Esperanto by M. Boirac, Rector of Dijon University and a noted Esperantist, who was amongst the French professors. Not understanding English, he was growing rather sleepy during a long speech, when the word "Esperanto" gave him a sudden shock. He thought the English official was poking fun at him, but was relieved to hear that the allusion had been sympathetic.

At this year's meeting of the Modern Language Society at Durham, the Warden of Durham University, Dean Kitchin, in welcoming the society to the town and university, gave considerable prominence in his speech to Esperanto, remarking that, to judge by its rapid growth and the sanity of its reformed grammar, one might easily believe that it will win general use.* Such references in high places illustrate the tendency to admit

* He continued : "To me it seems that Esperanto in vocabulary and grammar is a miracle of simplicity."

9

that there may be something in this international language scheme.

There are now (May 1907) seventy local Esperanto societies in Great Britain on the list of societies affiliated to the British Esperanto Association, and often several new ones are formed in a month. The first were Keighley and London, founded 1902. Seven more were formed in 1903; and since the beginning of 1906 no less than thirty-six. Besides the members of these there are a great many learners in classes and individual Esperantists who belong to no affiliated group. Every month one reads lists of lectures given in the most diverse places, very often with the note that a local club or class resulted, or that a large sale of Esperanto literature took place. Sometimes the immediate number of converts is surprising : e.g. on April 22, 1907, after a lecture on Esperanto at the Technical College, Darlington, seventy-eight students entered their names for a week's course of lessons to be held in the college three times a day.

There are now Esperanto consuls in the following towns: Bradford, Chester, Edinburgh, Harrogate, Hull, Hunslet, Keighley, Leeds, Liverpool, Nottingham, Oakworth, Plymouth, Rhos, Southampton, and St. Helens. Birmingham has within the last few months taken up the cause with its usual energy, and now has a large class.

In England the universities have been slow to show interest in Esperanto ; but now that Cambridge has been selected as the seat of the Congress in 1907, the university is granting every facility, as also is the town council, in use of rooms and the like, and some professors and other members of the university are cordially co-operating. Last October Prof. Skeat, one of the fathers of English philology, took the chair at a preliminary meeting, and made a speech very favourable to Esperanto. He said, " I think Esperanto is a very good movement, and I hope it will succeed." The subject of Esperanto is being well put before the teachers of Cambridgeshire, and the railway companies all over the country and abroad are granting special fares for the congress.* It is probable that the overwhelming demonstration of the possibilities of this international language will open the eyes of many who have hitherto been indifferent, and that the movement will enter on a new phase of expansion in England, and through the example of England, which is closely watched abroad, in the world at large.

IX

LESSONS TO BE DRAWN FROM THE FOREGOING HISTORY

THE extent to which more or less artificial languages are already used in various parts of the world for the transaction of inter-racial business, and the persistent preoccupation of thinkers with the idea for the last 200 years, culminating in the production of a great number of schemes in our own times, show that there *is* a demand for an international language, more perfect than has yet been available and universally valid. The list of languages proposed (see Part II., chap. ii.) by no means represents all that has been written and thought upon the subject. Many more have proposed solutions of the question, beginning with such men as Becher (1661), Kirchner (1665), Porele (1667), Upperdorf (1679), Müller (1681), Lobkowitz (1687), Besuier (1684), Solbrig (1725), Taboltzafo (1772), and continuing down to the present day. The striking success of Volapük and Esperanto in gaining, within a few years of publication, many thousands of ardent supporters has also been a revelation. It has proved most conclusively that there is a demand. If so many people in all lands have been willing to give up time and money to learning and promoting a language from which they could not expect to reap anything like full benefit for many years, what must be its value when ripened to yield full profits, i.e. when universally adopted ?

---

* It is a striking fact that six weeks before the opening of the congress 700 members have already secured their tickets.

There are two main obstacles to universal adoption. The first is common to all projects of reform—the force of inertia. It is hard to win practical support for a new thing, even when assent is freely given in theory to its utility. The second is peculiar to Esperanto, and consists in the discrediting of the cause of international language through the failure of Volapük. Good examples of its operation are afforded by the slowness of Germany to recognize Esperanto, and by the criticism of Prof. Münsterberg (formerly of Freiburg, Germany) in America, based as it is on an old German criticism of Volapük, and transferred at second-hand to Esperanto.

Hence every effort should be made to induce critics of Esperanto to examine the language before pronouncing judgment—to criticise the real thing, instead of some bogy of their imagination.

One bogy which has caused much misdirected criticism is raised by misunderstanding of the word "universal" in the phrase *universal language*. It is necessary to insist upon the fact that "universal" means universally adopted and everywhere current *as an auxiliary* to the mother-tongue for purposes of international communication. It does not mean a universal language for home consumption as a substitute for national language. In Baconian language, this bogy may be called an "idol of the market-place," since it rests upon confusion of terms.

Pursuing the Baconian classification of error, we may call the literary man's nightmare of the invasion of literature by the universal language an "idol of the theatre." The lesson of experience is, that it is well not to alienate the powerful literary interest justly concerned in upholding the dignity and purity of national speech by making extravagant claims on behalf of the auxiliary language. It is capable of conveying *matter* or *content* in any department of human activity with great nicety; but where it is a question of reproducing by actual translation the *form* or *manner* of some masterpiece of national literature, it will not, by nature of its very virtues, give a full idea of the rich play of varied synonymic in the original.

The great practical lesson of Volapük is, that alteration brings dissension, and dissension brings death. A universal language must be in essentials, like Esperanto, inviolable. If ever the time comes for modification in any essential point, it will be after official international recognition in the schools. Gradual reforms could then, if necessary, be introduced by authority, as in the case of the recent French " Tolérations," or the German reforms in orthography.

So long as the world is divided among rival great powers, no national language can be recognized as universal by them all. It is therefore a choice between an artificial language or nothing. As regards the structure of the artificial language itself, history shows clearly that it must be *a posteriori*, not *a priori*. It must select its constituent roots and its spoken sounds on the principle of maximum of internationality, and its grammar must be a simplification of natural existing grammar. On the other hand, a recent tendency to brand as "arbitrary" and *a priori* everything that makes for regularity, if it is not directly borrowed, is to be resisted. It is possible to overdo even the best of rules by slavish and unintelligent application. Thus it is urged by extremists that some of the neatest labour-saving devices of Esperanto are arbitrary, and therefore to be condemned.

Take the Esperanto suffix *-in-*, which denotes the feminine.

    "   "   prefix *mal-*   "   "   " opposite.

    "   "   suffix *-ig-*   "   " causative action.

Given the roots *bov-* (ox); *fort-* (strong); *grand-* (big): Esperanto forms *bovino* (cow); *malforta* (weak); *grandigi* (to augment); *malgrandigi* (to diminish).

These words are arbitrary, because not borrowed from national language. Let the public decide for itself whether it prefers a language which insists (in order not to be "arbitrary") upon borrowing fresh roots to express these ideas. Let any one who has learnt Latin, French, and German try how long it takes him to think of the masculine of *vacca*, *vache*, *Kuh* ; the opposite of *fortis*, *fort*, *stark* ; the Latin, French, and German ways of expressing " to make big" and " to make small." The issue is hardly doubtful.

Again, the languages upon whose vocabulary and grammar the international language is to be based must be Aryan (Indo-European). This is a practical point. The non-European peoples will consent to learn " simplified Aryan " just as they are adopting Aryan civilization ; but the converse is not true. The Europeans will go without an international language rather than learn one based to some extent upon Japanese or Mongolian. The only prescription for securing a large field is—greatest ease for greatest number, with a handicap in favour of Europeans, to induce them to enter.

PART III

THE CLAIMS OF ESPERANTO TO BE TAKEN SERIOUSLY : CONSIDERATIONS BASED ON THE STRUCTURE OF THE LANGUAGE ITSELF

I

ESPERANTO IS SCIENTIFICALLY CONSTRUCTED, AND FULFILS THE NATURAL TENDENCY IN EVOLUTION OF LANGUAGE

ALL national languages are full of redundant and overlapping grammatical devices for expressing what could be equally well expressed by a single uniform device. They bristle with irregularities and exceptions. Their forms and phrases are largely the result of chance and partial survival, arbitrary usage, and false analogy. It is obvious that a perfectly regular artificial language is far easier to learn. But the point to be insisted on here is, that artificial simplification of language is no fantastic craze, but merely a perfect realization of a natural tendency, which the history of language shows to exist.

At first sight this may seem to conflict with what was said in Part I., chap. x. But there is no real inconsistency. As pointed out there, there is no reason to think that Nature, left to herself, would ever produce a universal language, or that a simpler language would win, in a struggle with more complex ones, on account of its simplicity. But this does not prevent there being a real natural tendency to simplification—though in natural languages this tendency is constantly thwarted, and can never produce its full effect.

How, then, is this tendency to simplification shown in the

history of Aryan (Indo-European) languages? For it must be emphasized that for the purposes of this discussion history of language means history of Aryan language.

The Aryan group of languages includes Sanskrit and its descendants in the East, Greek, Latin, all modern Romance languages (French, Italian, Spanish, etc.), all Germanic languages (English, German, Scandinavian, etc.), all Slav languages (Russian, Polish, etc.)—in fact, all the principal languages of Europe, except Hungarian, Basque, and Finnish. The main tendency of this group of languages has been, technically speaking, to become analytic instead of synthetic—that is, to abandon complex systems of inflection by means of case and verbal endings, and to substitute prepositions and auxiliaries. Thus, taking Latin as the type of old synthetic Aryan language, its declension of nouns and conjugation of verbs present an enormously greater complexity of forms than are employed by English, the most advanced of the modern analytical languages, to express the same grammatical relations.   For example:

Nom.	*mensă*	= a table.	*mensae*	=	tables.
Acc.	*mensam*	= a table.	*mensas*	=	tables.
Gen.	*mensae*	= of a table.	*mensarum*	=	of tables.
Dat.	*mensae*	= { to or for a table.	*mensis*	=	to or for tables.
Abl.	*mensā*	= { by, with, or from a table.	*mensis*	=	{ by, with, or from tables.

By the time you have learnt these various Latin case endings (-*ă*, -*am*, -*ae*, -*ae*, -*ā* ; -*ae*, -*as*, -*arum*, -*is*, -*is*), you have only learnt one out of many types of declension. Passing on to the second Latin type or declension, e.g. *dominus* = master, you have to learn a whole fresh set of case endings (-*us*, -*um*, -*i*, -*o*, -*o* ; -*i*, -*os*, -*orum*, -*is*, -*is*) to express the same grammatical relations ; whereas in English you apply the same set of prepositions to the word " master " without change, except for a uniform -*s* in the plural. As there are a great many types of Latin noun, the simplification in English, effected by using invariable prepositions without inflection, is very great. It is just the same with the verb. Take the English regular verb " to love ": the four forms *love, loves, loving, loved*, about exhaust the number of forms to be learned (omitting the second person singular, which is practically dead) ; the rest is done by auxiliaries, which are the same for each verb. Latin, on the other hand, possesses very numerous forms of the verb, and the whole set of numerous forms varies for each type of verb. In the aggregate the simplification in English is enormous. This process of simplification is common to all the modern Aryan languages, but they have not all made equal progress in carrying it out.

Now, it is a remarkable fact, and a very suggestive one for those who seek to trace the connexion between the course of a nation's language and its history, that the degree of progress made by the languages of Europe along their common line of evolution does on the whole, as a matter of historical fact, correspond with the respective degree of material, social, and economic advancement attained by the nations that use them. Take this question of case endings. Russia has retained a high degree of inflection in her language, having seven cases with distinct endings. These seven cases are common to the Slav languages in general ; two of them (Sorbish and Slovenish) have, like Gothic and Greek, a dual number, a feature which has long passed away from the languages of Western Europe. Again, the Slav tongues decline many more of the numerals than most Aryan languages. Germany, which, until the recent formation of the German Empire, was undoubtedly a century slow by West European time, still has four cases ; or, in view of the moribund dative, should we rather say three and a half? France and England manage their affairs in a universal nominative * (if one can give any name to a universal case), as far as nouns, adjectives,

---

* Though historically, of course, the Low Latin universal case, from which many French, and therefore English, words are derived, was the accusative.

and articles are concerned. Their pronouns offer the sole survival of declension by case endings. Here France, the runner-up, is a trifle slow in the possession of a real, live dative case of the pronoun (acc. *le, la, les* ; dat. *lui, leur*). England wins by a neck with one universal oblique case (*him, her, them*). This insidious suggestion is not meant to endanger the *entente cordiale* ; even perfidious Albion would not convict the French nation of arrested development on the side-issue of pronominal atavism. Mark Twain says he paid double for a German dog, because he bought it in the dative case ; but no nation need be damned for a dative. We have no use for the *coup de Jarnac*.

But consider the article. Here, if anywhere, is a test of the power of a language to move with the times. For some reason or other (the real underlying causes of these changes in language needs are obscure) modern life has need of the article, though the highly civilized Romans did very well without it. So strong is this need that, in the middle ages, when Latin was used as an international language by the learned, a definite article (*hic* or τό) was foisted into the language. How is it with the modern world ? The Slavs have remained in this matter at the point of view of the ancient world. They are articleless. Germany has a cumbrous three-gender, four-case article ; France rejoices in a two-gender, one-case article with a distinct form for the plural. The ripe product of tendency, the infant heir of the eloquent ages, to whose birth the law of Aryan evolution groaned and travailed until but now, the most useful, if not the "mightiest," monosyllable "ever moulded by the lips of man," the "the," one and indeclinable, was born in the Anglo-Saxon mouth, and sublimed to its unique simplicity by Anglo-Saxon progress.

The general law of progress in language could be illustrated equally well from the history of genders as exhibited in various languages. We are here only dealing with Aryan languages, but, merely by way of illustration, it may be mentioned that a primitive African language offers seven "genders," or grammatical categories requiring the same kind of concords as genders. In

Europe we pass westward from the three genders of Germany, curving through feminine and masculine France (*place aux dames!*) to monogendric Britain. Only linguistic arbitrary gender is here referred to; this has nothing to do with suffragettes or "defeminization."

Again, take agreement of adjectives. In the ancient world, whether Greek, Latin, Gothic, or Anglo-Saxon, adjectives had to follow nouns through all the mazes of case and number inflection, and had also to agree in gender. In this matter German has gone ahead of French, in that its adjectives do not submit to change of form in order to indicate agreement, when they are used predicatively (e.g. "ein gut*er* Mann"; "der gut*e* Mann"; but "der Mann ist gut"). But English has distanced the field, and was alone in at the death of the old concords, which moistened our childhood's dry Latin *with* tears.

Whatever test be applied, the common tendency towards simplification, from synthesis to analysis, is there; and in its every manifestation English has gone farthest among the great literary languages. It is necessary to add this qualification—"among the great literary languages"—because, in this process of simplification, English has a very curious rival, and possibly a superior, in the *Taal* of South Africa. The curious thing is that a local dialect should have shown itself so progressive, seeing that the distinctive note of most dialects is conservatism, their chief characteristics being local survivals.* It is probable that the advanced degree of simplification attained by the Taal is the result of deliberate and conscious adaptation of their language by the original settlers to the needs of the natives. Just as Englishmen speak Pidgin-English to coolies in the East, so the old trekkers must have removed irregularities and concords from their

* Of course a difference must be expected between a dialect spoken by a miscellaneous set of settlers in a foreign land and one in use as an indigenous growth from father to son. But the *habitants*, as the French settlers in Quebec are called, who, like the Boers, are mainly a pastoral and primitive people, have retained an antiquated form of French, with no simplification.

Dutch, so that the Kaffirs could understand it. If this is so, it is another illustration of the essential feature that an international language must possess. Even the Boer farmers, under the stress of practical necessity, grasped the need of simplification.

The natural tendency towards elimination of exceptions is also strongly marked in the speech of the uneducated. Miss Loane, who has had life-long experience of nursing work among the poorest classes in England, tabulates (*The Queen's Poor*, p. 112) the points in which at the present day the language of the poor differs from that of the middle and upper classes. Under the heading of grammar she singles out specially superabundance of negatives, and then proceeds : "Other grammatical errors. These are nearly all on the lines of simplification. It is correct to say 'myself, herself, yourself, ourselves.' Very well : let us complete the list with 'hisself' and 'theirselves.' Most verbs are regular : why not all ? Let us say 'comed' and 'goed,' 'seed' and 'bringed' and 'teached.'" Miss Loane probably exaggerates with her "nearly all." For instance, as regards the uneducated form of the past tense of "to come," surely "come" is a commoner form than "comed." Similarly the illiterate for "I did" is "I done," not "I doed," which would be the regular simplification. But the natural tendency is certainly there, and it is strong.

Precisely the same tendency is observable in the present development of literary languages. They have all inherited many irregular verbal conjugations from the past as part of their national property, and these, by the nature of the case, comprise most of the commonest words in the language, because the most used is the most subject to abbreviation and modification. But these irregular types of inflection have long been dead, in the sense that they are fossilized survivals, incapable of propagating their kind. When a new word is admitted into the language, it is conjugated regularly. Thus, though we still say "I go—I went ; I run—I ran," because we cannot help ourselves, when we are free to choose we say, "I cycle—I cycled ; I wire—I wired"; just as the French say "télégraphier," and not "télégraphir," -oir, or -re.

Considering the strength of this stream of natural tendency, it seems a most natural thing to start again, for international purposes, with a form of simplified Aryan language, and, being free from the dead hand of the past, to set up the simplest forms of conjugation, etc., and make every word in the language conform to them.

Indeed, this question of artificial simplification of language has of late years emerged from the scholar's study and become a matter of practical politics, even as regards the leading national languages. Within the last few years there have been official edicts in France and Germany, embodying reforms either in spelling or grammar, with the sole object of simplifying. The latest attempt at linguistic jerrymandering has been the somewhat autocratic document of President Roosevelt. He has found that there are limits to what the American people will stand even from him, and it seems likely to remain a dead letter. But there is not the smallest doubt that the English language is heavily handicapped by its eccentric vowel pronunciation and its spelling that has failed to keep pace with the development of the language. The same is true, though in a lesser degree, of the spelling and pronunciation of French. Since the whole theory of spelling— and, until a few hundred years ago, its practice too—consisted in nothing else but an attempt to represent simply and accurately the spoken word, most unprejudiced people would admit that simplification is in principle advisable. But the practical difficulties in the way of simplification of a national language are almost prohibitive. It is hard to see that there are any such obstacles in the way of the adoption of a simple and perfectly phonetic international artificial language. We dislike change because it is change, and new things because they are new. We go on suffering from a movable Easter, which most practically inconveniences great numbers of people and interests, and seems to benefit no one at all, simply because it is no one's business to change it. If once the public could be got to examine seriously the case for an artificial international language, they could hardly fail to recognize what an easy, simple, and *natural* thing it is, and how soon it would pay off all capital sunk in its universal adoption, and be pure profit.

NOTE

This seems the best place to deal with a criticism of Esperanto which has an air of plausibility. It is urged that Esperanto does not carry the process of simplification far enough, and that in two important points it shows a retrograde tendency to revert to a more primitive stage of language, already left behind by the most advanced natural languages. These points are :

(1) The possession of an accusative case.
(2) The agreement of adjectives.

Now, it must be borne in mind that the business of a universal language is, not to adhere pedantically to any philological theory, not to make a fetish of principle, not to strive after any theoretical perfection in the observance of certain laws of construction, but—simply to be easy. The principle of simplification is an admirable one, because it furthers this end, and for this reason only. The moment it ceases to do so, it must give way before a higher canon, which demands that an international language shall offer the greatest ease, combined with efficiency, for the greatest number. The fact that a scientific study of language reveals a strong natural tendency towards simplification, and that this tendency has in certain languages assumed certain forms, is not in itself a proof that an artificial language is bound to follow the historical lines of evolution in every detail. It will follow them just so far as, and no farther than, they conduce to its paramount end—greatest ease for greatest number, plus maximum of efficiency. In constructing an international language, the question then becomes, in each case that comes up for decision : How far does the proposed simplification conduce to ease without sacrificing efficiency? Does the cost of retention (reckoned in terms of sacrifice of ease) of the unsimplified form outweigh the advantages (reckoned in terms of efficiency) it confers, and which would be lost if it was simplified out of existence? Let us then examine briefly the two points criticised, remembering that the main function of the argument from history of language is, not to deduce therefrom hard-and-fast rules for the construction of international language, but to remove the unreasoning prejudice of numerous objectors, who cannot pardon the international language for being "artificial," i.e. consciously simplified.

(1) *The Accusative Case*

This is formed in Esperanto by adding the letter *-n*. This one form is universal for nouns, adjectives, and pronouns singular and plural. Ex.:

Nom. *bona patro* (good father), plural, *bonaj patroj.*
Acc. *bonan patron*   „   *bonajn patrojn.*

Suppose one were to suppress this *-n*.

(*a*) Cost of retention of unsimplified form: Remembering to add this *-n*.

(*b*) Advantages of retention: The flexibility of the language is enormously increased; the words can be put in any order without obscuring or changing the sense. Ex.:

La patro amas sian filon = the father loves his son.

Sian filon amas la patro (in English "his son loves the father" has a different sense).

Amas la patro sian filon (= the father *loves* his son, but . . .).

La patro sian filon amas.

Sian filon la patro amas (= it is his son that the father loves).

In every case the Esperanto sentence is perfectly clear, the meaning is the same, but great scope is afforded for emphasis and shades of gradation. Further, every nation is enabled to arrange the words as suits it best, without becoming less intelligible to other nations. Readers of Greek and Latin know the enormous advantage of free word order. For purposes of rendering the spirit and swing of national works of literature in Esperanto, and for facilitating the writing of verse, the accusative is a priceless boon. Is the price too high?

N.B.—Those people who are most apt to omit the -*n* of the accusative, having no accusative in their own language, generally make their meaning perfectly clear without it, because they are accustomed to indicate the objective case by the order in which they place their words. They make a mistake of Esperanto by omitting the -*n*, but they are understood, which is the essential.

(2) *The Agreement of Adjectives*

Adjectives in Esperanto agree with their substantives in number and case. Ex.: *bona patro, bonan patron, bonaj patroj, bonajn patrojn.*

Suppose one were to suppress agreement of adjectives.

(*a*) Cost of retention of agreement: Remembering to add -*j* for the plural and -*n* for the accusative.

(*b*) Advantages of retention: Greater clearness; conformity with the usage of the majority of languages; euphony.

Esperanto has wisely adopted full, vocalic, syllabic endings for words. Contrast Esp. *bon-o* with French *bon*, Eng. *good*, Germ. *gut.* By this means Esperanto is not only rendered slower, more harmonious, and easier of comprehension; it is also able to denote the parts of speech clearly to eye and ear by their form. Thus final -*o* bespeaks a noun; -*a*, an adjective; -*e*, an adverb; -*i*, an infinitive, etc.

Now, since all adjectives end in syllabic -*a*, it is much harder to keep them uninflected than if they ended with a consonant like the Eng. "good." To talk about *bona patroj* would not only seem a hideous barbarism to all Latin peoples, whose languages Esperanto most resembles, but it would also offend the bulk of Northerners. After a very little practice it is really easier to say *bonaj patroj* than *bona patroj*. The assimilation of termination tempts the ear and tongue.

The grammar is also simplified. For if adjectives agreeing with nouns and pronouns expressed were invariable, it would probably be necessary to introduce special rules to meet the case of adjectives standing as nouns, or where the qualified word was suppressed.

Again, is the price too high compared to the advantages?

II

ESPERANTO FROM AN EDUCATIONAL POINT OF VIEW—IT WILL AID THE LEARNING OF OTHER LANGUAGES AND STIMULATE INTELLIGENCE

(1) ESPERANTO takes a natural place at the beginning of the sequence of languages, upon which is founded the scheme of language-teaching in the Reform Schools of Germany, and in some of the more progressive English schools.

The principle involved in this scheme is that of orderly progression from the easier to the more difficult. Only one foreign language is begun at a time. The easiest language in the school curriculum is begun first. Enough hours per week are devoted to this language to allow of decent progress being made. When the pupils have a fair grip of the elements of one language, another is begun. The bulk of the school language-teaching hours are now devoted to the new language, and sufficient weekly hours are given to the language already learnt to avoid backsliding at least. Thus in a German school of the new type the linguistic hours are devoted in the lowest classes to the mother-tongue. When the pupils have some idea what language means, and have acquired some notion of grammar, they are given a school year or two of French. After this Latin is begun in the upper part of the school, and Greek at a corresponding interval after Latin.

Now, it is one of the commonest complaints of teachers in our secondary schools that they have to begin teaching Latin or

French to boys who have no knowledge whatever of grammar. Fancy the hopelessness of trying to teach an English boy the construction of a Latin or French sentence when he does not know what a relative or demonstrative pronoun means! This is the fate of so many a master that quite a number of them resign themselves to giving up a good part of their French or Latin hour to endeavouring to imbue their flock with some notions of grammar in general. They naturally try to appeal to their boys through the medium of their own language. But those who have incautiously upset their class from the frying-pan of *qui, quae, quod*, into the fire of English demonstrative and relative pronouns get a foretaste of the fire that dieth not. *Facilis descensus Averni.* Happy if they do not lose heart, and step downward from the fire to ashes—reinforced with sackcloth.

"I contend that that 'that' that that gentleman said was right." This is the "abstract and brief chronicle" of their woes—sometimes, indeed, the epitaph of their pedagogical career, if they are too sickened of the Sisiphean task of trying to teach grammar on insufficient basis. And this use, or abuse, of the hardworked word "that" is only an extreme case which illustrates the difficulty of teaching grammar to babes, through the medium of a language honeycombed with synonyms, homonyms, exceptions, and other pitfalls (can you be honeycombed with a pitfall?)—a language which seems to take a perverse delight in breaking all its own rules and generally scoring off the beginner. And for the dull beginner, what language does not seem to conform to this type? Answer: Esperanto.

In other words, it would seem that, for the grinding of grammar and the advancement of sound learning in the initial stage, there is nothing like an absolutely uniform and regular language,* a

---

* Cf. Sir Oliver Lodge : "It would certainly appear that for this purpose [i.e. educative language-learning for children] the fully inflected ancient languages are best and most satisfactory ; if they were still more complete and regular, like Esperanto, they would be better still to begin with" (*School Teaching and School Reform*, p. 21 : chapter on Curricula and Methods).

type tongue, something that corresponds in the linguistic hierarchy to Euclid or the first rules of arithmetic in the mathematical, something clear, consistent, self-evident, and of universal application.

Take our sentence again : " I contend that that 'that' that that gentleman said was right." If our beginner has imbibed his first notions of grammar through the medium of a type language, in which a noun is always a noun, and is stamped as such by its form (this, by the way, is an enormous aid in making the thing clear to children); in which an adjective is always an adjective, and is stamped as such by its form ; and so on through all the other parts of speech,—when the teacher comes to analyse the sentence given, he will be able to explain it by reference to the known forms of the regular key-language. He will point out that of the "thats": the first is the Esperanto *ke* (which is final, because *ke* never means anything else) ; the second is *tiu* (at once revealed by its form to be a demonstrative), the fourth *kiu*, and so on. As for the third " that," which *is* rather hard for a child to grasp, he will be able to make it into a noun in form by merely adding *-o* to the Esperanto equivalent for any "that" required. He will not be doing violence to the language ; for Esperanto consists of roots, which habitually do duty as noun, verb, adjective, etc., according to the termination added. Those who know the value of the concrete and tangible in dealing with children will grasp the significance of the new possibilities that are thus for the first time opened up to language-teachers.

To sum up : Natural languages are all hard, and the beginner can never go far enough to get a rule fixed soundly in his mind without meeting exceptions which puzzle and confuse him. Esperanto is as clear, logical, and consistent as arithmetic, and, like arithmetic, depends more upon intelligence than upon memory work. If Esperanto were adopted as the first foreign language to be taught in schools, and all grammatical teaching were postponed until Esperanto had been begun, and then given entirely through the medium of Esperanto until a sound notion of grammatical rules and categories had been instilled, it would probably be found that the subsequent task of learning natural languages would be facilitated and abridged. From the very start it would be possible to prevent certain common errors and confusions, that tend to become engrained in juvenile minds by the fluctuating or contradictory usage of their own language, to their great let and hindrance in the subsequent stages of language-learning. The skeleton outline of grammatical theory with concrete examples afforded by Esperanto would shield against vitiating initial mistakes, in much the same way as the use of a scientific phonetic alphabet, when a foreign language is presented for the first time to the English beginner in written form, shields him against carrying over his native mixed vowel system to languages which use the same letters as English, but give quite a different value to them. In both cases * the essentials of the new instrument of learning are the same—that it be of universal application, that it be sufficiently different from the mother-tongue or alphabet to prevent confusion by association of ideas, that each of the new forms or letters convey only one idea or sound respectively, and that this idea or sound be always and only conveyed by that form or letter.

(2) From a psychological point of view Esperanto would be·a rewarding subject of study for children.

The above remarks on sequence of languages show that, by placing Esperanto first in the language curriculum, justice is done to the psychological maxim : from the easier to the harder, from the regular to the exceptional. It may further be argued (a) that Esperanto is educative in the real sense of the word, i.e. suitable for drawing out and developing the reasoning powers ; (b) that it would act as a stimulus, and by its ease set a higher standard of attainment in language-learning.

(a) Amidst all the discussion of "educationists" about methods, curricula, sequence of studies, and the rest, one

* i.e. scientific regular type grammar and scientific regular phonetic alphabet.

fundamental fact continues to face the teacher when he gets down to business; and that is, that he has got to make the taught think for themselves. In proportion as his teaching makes them contribute their share of effort will it be fruitful. This is, of course, the merest truism, sometimes dignified in the current pedagogical slang by the name of "self-activity," or the like. But whatever new bottles the theorists, and their extreme left wing the faddists, may choose to serve up our old wine in, the fact is there: children have got to be made to use their own brains. The eternal question that faces the teacher is, how to provide problems that children really can work out by using their own brains. The trouble about history, geography, English literature, and such subjects is that the subject-matter of the problems they offer for solution lies beyond the experience of the young, and to a large extent beyond their reasoning powers. In teaching all such subjects there is accordingly the perpetual danger that the real work done may degenerate into mere memory work, or parrot-like cramming of notes or dates.

The same difficulty is encountered in science teaching. Heuristic methods have been devised to meet the difficulty. Though they are no doubt psychologically sound, they tend to be very slow in results; hence the common jibe that a boy may learn as much by them in five years as he could learn out of a a shilling text-book in a term.

The old argument that "mental gymnastics" are best supplied by Latin is sound to the extent that Latin really does furnish a perpetual series of small problems that have to be solved by the aid of grammar and dictionary, but which do involve real mental effort, since mere mechanical looking out of words does not suffice for their elucidation. But for various reasons, such as the remoteness of the ancient world in time, place, modes of thought, etc., Latin tends to be too hard and not interesting enough for the average boy. He gets discouraged, and develops a habit of only working enough to keep out of trouble with the school authorities, and is apt to leave school with an unintelligent attitude towards intellectual things in general. This is the result of early drudging at a subject in which progress is very slow, and which by its nature is uncongenial. The great desideratum is a linguistic subject which shall at once inculcate a feeling for language (German *Sprachgefühl*), and yet be easy enough to admit of rapid progress. Nothing keeps alive the quickening zest that makes learning fruitful like the consciousness of making rapid progress.

Hitherto arithmetic and Euclid have been the ideal subjects for providing the kind of problem required—one that can be worked out with certainty by the aid of rule and use of brain, without calling for knowledge or experience that the child cannot have. The facts are self-evident, and follow from principles, without involving any extraneous acquaintance with life or literature, and no deadening memory work is required. If only there were some analogous subject on the literary side, to give a general grip of principles, uncomplicated by any arbitrary element, what a boon it would be! and what a sound preparation for real and more advanced linguistic study for those who showed aptitude for this line! Arithmetic and Euclid both really depend upon common sense; but partly owing to their abstract nature, and partly because they are always classed as "mathematics," they seem to contain something repellent to many literary or linguistic types of mind.

With the invention of a perfectly regular and logically constructed language, a concrete embodiment of the chief principles of language structure, we have offered us for the first time the hitherto missing linguistic equivalent of arithmetic or Euclid. In a regular language, just because everything goes by rule, problems can be set and worked out analogous to sums in arithmetic and riders in Euclid. Given the necessary roots and rules, the learner can manufacture the necessary vocabulary and produce the answer with the same logical inevitability; and he has to use his brains to apply his rules, instead of merely copying words out of a dictionary, or depending upon his memory for them.

In this way all that part of language-study which tends to be dead weight in teaching the young is got rid of in one fell swoop, and this though the language taught and learnt is a highly developed instrument for reading, writing, speaking, and literary expression. This dead weight includes most of the unintelligent memorizing, all exceptions, all complicated systems of declension and conjugation, all irregular comparison of adjectives and adverbs, all syntactical subtleties (cf. the sequence of tenses, oratio obliqua, the syntax of subordinate clauses, in Latin ; and the famous conditional sentences, with the no less notorious οὐ and μή in Greek), all conflicting and illogical uses of auxiliaries (cf. *être* and *avoir* in French, and *sein* and *haben* in German), besides a host of other old enemies. Some of these things of course are not wholly memory work, especially the syntax, which involves a real feeling for language. But these would be much better postponed until one easy foreign language has been learnt thoroughly. Every multilinguist knows that each foreign language is easier to learn than the last. With a perfectly regular artificial language you can make so much progress in a short time that you can use it freely for practical purposes. Yet it does not come of itself, like the mother-tongue. *This free manipulation of a consciously acquired language is the very best training for forming a feeling for language*—far better than weary stumbling over the baby stages of a hard language. When you can read, write, and speak one very easy artificial language, which you have had to learn as a foreign one, then is the time when you can profitably tackle the difficulties of natural language, appreciating the niceties of syntax, and realizing, by comparison with your normal key-language, in what points natural languages are merely arbitrary and have to be learnt by heart. Those who have early conquered the grammar and syntax of any foreign language, but have had to put in years of hard (largely memory) work before they could write or speak, e.g., Latin Latin, French French, or German German, will realize the saving effected, when they are told that Esperanto has no idiom, no arbitrary usage. The combination of words is not governed, as in natural languages, by tradition (which tradition has to be assimilated in the sweat of the brow), but is free, the only limits being common sense, common grammar, and lucidity.

To those who do not know Esperanto it may seem a dark saying that language riders can be worked out in the same way as geometrical ones. To understand this some knowledge of the language is necessary (for sample problems see Appendix A, p. 200). But for the sake of making the argument intelligible it may here be stated that one of the labour-saving, vocabulary-saving devices of Esperanto is the employment of a number of suffixes with fixed meaning, that can be added to any root. Thus:

> The suffix *-ej-* denotes place.
>   ,,   ,,   *-il-*   ,,   instrument.
>   ,,   ,,   *-ig-*   ,,   causation.
> Final *-o* denotes a noun.

Given this and the root *san-* (cf. Lat. *sanus*), containing the idea of health, form words for "to heal" (*san-ig-i* = to cause to be well) ; " medicine " (*san-ig-il-o* = instrument of healing) ; "hospital" (*san-ig-ej-o* = place of healing), etc.

This is merely an example. The combinations and permutations are infinite ; they give a healthy knowledge of word-building, and can be used in putting whole pages of carefully prepared idiomatic English into Esperanto. Practical experience shows that, given the necessary crude roots, the necessary suffixes, and a one-page grammar of the Esperanto language, an intelligent person can produce in Esperanto a translation of a page of idiomatic English, not Ollendorfian phrases, *without having learnt Esperanto*.

(*b*) Experience also shows that the intelligent one thoroughly enjoys himself while doing so ; and having done so, experiences a thrill of exhilaration almost amounting to awe at having made a better translation into a language he has never learnt than he could make into a national language that he has learnt for years, e.g. Latin, French, or German.

And what is exhilaration in the dry tree may be sustained working keenness in the green. The stimulus to the young mind of progress swift and sure is immense. A child who has learnt to read, write, and speak Esperanto in six months, as is very possible within the natural limits of power of expression imposed by his age, not only has a sound working knowledge of grammatical categories and forms, which will stand him in good stead in subsequent language-learning; he has also a quite different attitude of mind—*une tout autre mentalité*, to use recent jargon—towards foreign languages. His only experience of learning one has been that he did so with the object and result of being able to read, write, and speak it within a reasonable time. "By so much the greater and more resounding the slump into actuality," you will say, "when he comes to grapple with his next." Perhaps. But even so, the habit of acquiring fresh words and forms for immediate use must surely tell—not to mention that he will incidentally have acquired a very useful Romance vocabulary, and a wholly admirable French lucidity of construction.

(3) And this question of lucidity brings us to the third great educational advantage of Esperanto. Its opponents—without having ever learnt it to see—have urged that its preciseness will debauch the literary sense. Surely the exact opposite is the fact. *Le style c'est l'homme*, and the essence of true style is that a man should give accurate expression to his thoughts. The French wit, satirizing vapid fine writing, said that language was given to man to enable him to conceal his thought. There is no more potent instrument for obscuring or concealing thought than the ready-made phrase. Take up many a piece of journalese or other slipshod writing, and note how often the conventional phrase or word slips from under the pen, meaning nothing in particular. The very conventionality disguises from writer and reader the confusion or absolute lack of idea it serves to cloak. Both are lulled by the familiar sound of the set phrase or word and glide easily over them. On the other hand, in using a language in which you construct a good deal of your vocabulary

according to logical rule *tout en marchant*, it is impossible to avoid thinking, at each moment, exactly what you do mean. Where there is no idiom, no arbitrary usage, no ready-made phrase, there is also far less danger of yielding to a fatal facility.

Take an instance or two. In the Prayer Book occurs the phrase "Fulfil, O Lord, our desires and petitions." At Sunday lunch a mixed party of people, after attending morning service, were asked how they would render into Esperanto the word "desires." They nearly all plumped for *dezirajo*. Now, the Esperanto root for "desire" is *dezir-*. By adding *-o* it becomes a noun = the act of desiring, a desire. By adding the suffix *-aj*, and then *-o*, it becomes concrete = a desire- (i.e. desired-) thing, a desire. A reference to the dictionary showed that the English word "desire" has both these meanings, but none of these people had a sufficiently accurate idea of the use of language to realize this. It was only when a gentleman passed his plate for a second helping of beef, and was asked which he expected to be fulfilled— the beef, or his aspiration for beef—that he, under the stimulus of hunger, adopted the rendering *dezir-o*, thereby saving at once his bacon and his additional beef.

It is not of course necessary for people to define pedantically to themselves the meaning of every word they use, but surely it must conduce to clear thinking to use a language in which you are perpetually called upon, if you are writing seriously, to make just the mental effort necessary to think what you do mean.

Again, consider the use of prepositions. This is, in nearly all national languages, extremely fluctuating and arbitrary. Take a few English phrases showing the use of the prepositions "at" and "with." "At seven o'clock"; "at any price"; "at all times"; "at the worst"; "let it go at that"; "I should say at a guess," etc. "Come with me"; "write with a pen"; "he came with a rush"; "things are different with us"; "with a twinkle in his eye"; "with God all things are possible," etc. Try to turn these phrases into any language you think you know; the odds are that you will find yourself "up against it pretty badly." The fact is, that prepositions are very frequently used on no logical plan, not at all according to any fixed or universal meaning ; all that can be said about them in a given phrase is that they are used there because they are used.   To remember their equivalents in other languages hard memory work and much phrase-learning is necessary.   In Esperanto all that is necessary is : first, to become clear as to the exact meaning ; secondly, to pick the preposition that conveys it. There is no doubt, as the Esperanto prepositions are fixed in sense, on the " one word one meaning " plan.   The point is, that there is no memory searching, often so utterly vain, for there are few people indeed who can write a few pages of the most familiar foreign languages without getting their prepositions all wrong, and having " foreigner " stamped large all across their efforts.   In Esperanto, provided you have a clear mind and know your grammar, *you are right*.   No arbitrary usage defeats your efforts and makes discouraging jargon of your literary attempts.

This training in clear thought, the first requisite for all good writing, is surely sound practical pedagogics.   By the time you can give up conscious word-building in Esperanto, and use words and phrases by rote, you have done enough bracing thinking to teach you caution in the use of the ready-made phrase and horror of the vague word.

Fools make phrases, and wise men shun them.   Here is a phrase-free language : need we shun it ?

III

COMPARATIVE TABLES ILLUSTRATING LABOUR SAVED IN LEARNING
ESPERANTO AS CONTRASTED WITH OTHER LANGUAGES

(*a*) WORD-BUILDING

THE following tables are meant to give some idea of the number and variety of different ideas that can be expressed by a single Esperanto root, with the addition of affixes (prefixes and suffixes). By reading the English, French, and German columns downwards,

Affix	Esperanto	English	French	German
	san-a	healthy	bien portant	gesund
mal- (opposite)	mal-san-a	ill	malade	krank
ne (not)	ne-san-a	unwell	(un peu) souf-frant	unwohl
-ig (causative)	san-ig-i	to heal	guérir	heilen
	san-ig-a	salutary	salutaire	heilsam
re- (again)	re-san-ig-a	restorative	restaurant	wiederherste lend
-iĝ (becoming)	san-iĝ-i	to be conval-escent	être conval-escent	sich erholen
-ig	re-san-iĝ-a	getting well again	en train de se rétablir	genesend
-iĝ	mal-san-ig-a	sickening (transitive)	écoeurant (qui rend malade)	ekelhaft (krank machend
	mal-san-iĝ-a	sickening (intransitive)	languissant	siechend
-ist (agent)	san-ig-ist-o	doctor	médecin	Arzt
-ej (place)	san-ig-ej-o	hospital	hôpital	Krankenha
-ul (character-istic)	mal-san-ul-o	invalid	un malade	ein Kranke
-ebl (possibility)	(mal)-san-ig-ebl-a	(in)curable	(in)curable	(un)heilbar
-ar (collective)	mal-san-ul-ar-o	hospital in-mates	ensemble des malades	Gesamtheit Kranken
ge- (both sexes)	ge-mal-san-ul-ar-o	all the men and women patients	les malades hommes et femmes	die Kran beider schlechte
-in (feminine)	san-ig-ist-in-o	a lady doctor	un médecin femme	Arztin
-edz (married)	san-ig-ist-edz in-o	a doctor's wife	une femme de médecin	Frau des Ar

Affix	Esperanto	English	French	German
	lern-i	to learn	apprendre	lernen
(causative)	lern-ig-i	to teach	enseigner	lehren
	lern-ig-a	educative	éducateur	erzieherisch
(place)	lernej-o	school	école	Schule
t (pres. part.)	lern-ant-o	pupil	élève	Schüler
(of both sexes)	ge-lern-ant-oj	pupils of both sexes	élèves des deux sexes	Schüler and Schülerinnen
(collective)	lern-ant-ar-o	class	classe	Klasse
ppertaining)	lern-ej-an-o	schoolboy	écolier	Schulknabe
(feminine)	lern - ej-an - in-o	schoolgirl	écolière	Schulmädchen
r (chief)	lern-ej-estr-o	headmaster	proviseur	Direktor
(agent)	lern-ej-ist-o	schoolmaster	instituteur (professeur)	Lehrer
	lern-ej-ist-in-o	school-mistress	institutrice	Lehrerin
(concrete)	lern-aĵ-o	subject (learnt-stuff)	matière d'enseignement	Lehrstoff
	lern-aĵ-ar-o	curriculum	ensemble des matières d'enseigne-ment	(Studien)-Laufbahn Schulprogramm
nclination)	lern-em-a	studious	appliqué	fleissig
(opposite)	mal-lern-em-a	idle	paresseux	faul
causative)	lern-em-ig-i	to stimulate	mettre en train	anregen
	lern-ig-o	instruction (act)	instruction	das Unter-richten
	lern-ig-aĵ-o	instruction (teaching given)	enseignement	Unterricht

the reader will see how many different roots and periphrases these languages employ in order to express the same ideas.

As the affixes have fixed meanings, they only have to be learnt once for all, and many of them (e.g. *-ist*, *-in*, *re-*) are already familiar. When once acquired, they can be used in unending permutation and combination with different roots and each other. The tables below are by no means exhaustive of what can be done with the roots *san-* and *lern-*. They are merely illustrative. By referring to the full table of affixes on pp. 191-2, the reader can go on forming new compounds *ad libitum*: e.g. san-o, san-a, san-e, san-i, saneco, sanilo, sanulo, malsane, malsani, saneti, malsaneti, sanadi, eksani, eksaniĝi, saninda, sanindi, sanindulo, sanaĵo, sanaĵero, sanilo, sanigilo, sanigilejo, sanigilujo, sanigilisto, malsanemeco, remalsano, remalsanigo, sanila, malsanulino, sanistinedzo, sanilingo, sanigestro, sanigestrino, sanigema, sanega, sanigega, gesanantoj, saniĝontoj, sanigistido, sanigejano . . . and so on (kaj tiel plu).

(*b*) PARTICIPLES AND AUXILIARIES

The following table (see p. 160) illustrates the perfect simplicity and terseness of the Esperanto verb.

Every tense, active and passive, is formed with never more than two words. Every shade of meaning (continued, potential, etc., action) is expressed by these two words, of which one is the single auxiliary *esti* (itself conjugated regularly). The double auxiliary—" to be" and " to have"—which infests most modern languages, with all its train of confusing and often illogical distinctions (cf. French *je suis allé*, but *j'ai couru*), disappears. Contrast the simplicity of *amota* with the cumbersome periphrasis *about to be loved*; or the perfect ease and clearness of *vi estus amita* with the treble-barrelled German *Sie würden geliebt worden sein*.

This simplicity of the Esperanto verb is entirely due to its full participial system. There are six participles, present, past, and future active and passive, each complete in one word. The only natural Aryan language (of those commonly studied) that compares with Esperanto in this respect is Greek; and it is precisely the fulness of the Greek participial system that lends to the language a great part of that flexibility which all ages have agreed in admiring in it pre-eminently. Take a page of Plato or any other Greek author, and count the number of participles and note their use. They will be found more numerous and more delicately effective than in other languages. Esperanto can do all this; and it can do it without any of the complexity of form and irregularity that makes the learning of Greek verbs such a hard task. Bearing in mind the three characteristic vowels of the three tenses—present -a, past -i, future -o (common to finite tenses and participles)—the proverbial schoolboy, and the dullest at that, could hardly make the learning of the Esperanto participles last him half an hour.

It would be easy to go on filling page after page with the simplifications effected by Esperanto, but these will not fail to strike the learner after a very brief acquaintance with the language. But attention ought to be drawn to one more particularly clever device—the form of asking questions. An Esperanto statement is converted into a question without any inversion of subject and verb or any change at all, except the addition of the interrogative particle *ĉu*. In this Esperanto agrees with Japanese. But whereas Japanese adds its particle *ka* at the end of the sentence, the Esperanto *ĉu* stands first in its clause. Thus when, speaking Esperanto, you wish to ask a question, you begin by shouting out *ĉu*, an admirably distinctive monosyllable which cannot be confused with any other word in the language. By this means you get your interlocutor prepared and attending, and you can then frame your question at leisure.

Contrast Esperanto and English in the ease with which they respectively convert a statement into a question.

English : You went—did you go ?
Esperanto : Vi iris—ĉu vi iris ?

Esperanto	English	French	German
amanta	loving	aimant	liebend
aminta	having loved	ayant aimé	der geliebt hat
amonta	about to love	devant aimer	der lieben wird
amata	being loved	étant aimé	der geliebt wird
amita	(having been) loved	(ayant été) aimé	der geliebt worden ist
amota	about to be loved	devant être aimé	der geliebt werden soll
mi estas aminta	I have loved	j'ai aimé	ich habe geliebt
vi estis aminta	you had loved	vous aviez aimé	Sie hatten geliebt
li estas amanta	he is loving	il est aimant	er ist liebend
ŝi estis amata	she was being loved	elle était en train d'être aimée	sie war im Zuge geliebt zu werden
ni estos amintaj	we shall have loved	nous aurons aimé	wir werden geliebt haben
vi estas amataj	you are loved	vous êtes aimés	Sie werden geliebt
ili estas amitaj	they have been loved	ils ont été aimés	sie sind geliebt worden
mi estus aminta	I should have loved	j'aurais aimé	ich würde geliebt haben
vi estus amita	you would have been loved	vous auriez été aimé	Sie würden geliebt worden sein
li estas foririnta	he has gone away	il s'en est allé	er ist fortgegangen
ili estus foririntaj	they would have gone away	ils s'en seraient allés	sie würden fortgegangen sein

This particle may be considered the equivalent of the initial mark of interrogation used in Spanish, and serves to remove all complications in connexion with word order.

This chapter on labour-saving may fitly conclude with an estimate of the amount of mere memorizing work to be done in Esperanto. Since this is almost *nil* for grammar, syntax, and idiom, and since there are no irregularities or exceptions, the memory work is, broadly speaking, reduced to learning the affixes, the table of correlatives, and a certain number of new roots. This number is astonishingly small. Here is an estimate made by Prof. Macloskie, of Princeton, U.S.A.:

Number of roots new to an English boy without Latin, about 600*
  ,,   ,,   ,,   ,,   ,, with ,, ,, 300
  ,,   ,,   ,, a college teacher .   .   . 100

IV

HOW ESPERANTO CAN BE USED AS A CODE LANGUAGE TO COMMUNICATE WITH PERSONS WHO HAVE NEVER LEARNT IT

TECHNICALLY speaking, Esperanto combines the characteristics of an inflected language with those of an agglutinative one. This means that the syllables used as inflexions (*-o, -a, -e, -as, -is, -os, -ant-, -int-, -ont-*, etc.), being invariable and of universal application, can also be regarded as separate words. And as separate words they all figure in the dictionary, under their initial letters. Thus anything written in Esperanto can be deciphered by the simple process of looking out words and parts of words in the dictionary. For examples, see pieces 1 and 2 in the specimens of Esperanto, pp. 167-8, and read the Note at the beginning of Part IV. As the Esperanto dictionary only consists

* i.e. about one-third of the whole number in the *Fundamento*.

of a few pages, it can be easily carried in the pocket-book or waistcoat pocket.

Thus, while to the educated person of Aryan speech Esperanto presents the natural appearance of an ordinary inflected language, one who belongs by speech to another lingual family, or any one who has never heard of Esperanto, can regard every inflected word as a compound of invariable elements. By turning over very few pages he can determine the meaning and use of each element, and therefore, by putting them together, he can arrive at the sense of the compound word. e.g. *lav'ist'in'o*. Look out *lav-*, and you find "wash"; look out *-ist*, and you find it expresses the person who does an action; look out *-in*, and you find it expresses the feminine; look out *-o*, and you find it denotes a noun. Put the whole together, and you get "female who does washing, laundress."

Suppose you are going on an ocean voyage, and you expect to be shut up for weeks in a ship with persons of many nationalities. You take with you keys to Esperanto, price one halfpenny each, in various languages. You wish to tackle a Russian. Write your Esperanto sentence clearly and put the paper in his hand. At the same time hand him a Russian key to Esperanto, pointing to the following paragraph (in Russian) on the outside :

"Everything written in the international language can be translated by the help of this vocabulary. If several words together express but a single idea, they are written in one word, but separated by apostrophes; e.g. *frat'in'o*, though a single idea, is yet composed of three words, which must be looked for separately in the vocabulary."

After he has got over his shock of surprise, your Russian, if a man of ordinary education, will make out your sentence in a very short time by using the key.

As an example Dr. Zamenhof gives the following sentence: 'Mi ne sci'as kie mi las'is la baston'o'n: ĉu vi ĝi'n ne vid'is?" With the vocabulary this sentence will work out as follows :

Mi	*mi* = **I**	**I**
ne	*ne* = not	not
sci'as	{ *sci* = know { *as* = sign of present tense	} do know
kie	*kie* = where	where
mi	*mi* = **I**	I
las'is	{ *las* = leave { *is* = sign of past tense	} have left
la	*la* = the	the
baston'o'n	{ *baston* = stick { *o* = sign of a noun { *n* = sign of objective case	} stick
ĉu	*ĉu* = whether, sign of question	whether
vi	*vi* = you	you
ĝi'n	{ *ĝi* = it { *n* = sign of objective case	} it
ne	*ne* = not	not
vid'is	{ *vid* = see { *is* = sign of past tense	} have seen ?

It is obvious that no natural language can be used in the same way as a code to be deciphered with a small key.

German		French	
Ich	I	*je*	**I**
weiss	white	*ne*	not
nicht	not	*sais*	?
wo	where	*pas*	step
ich	I	*où*	where
den	?	*j'ai*	?
Stock	stick	*laissé*	?
gelassen	dispassionate	*la*	the
habe :	property :	*canne :*	reed :
haben	to have	*ne*	not
Sie	she, they, you,	*l'avez*	?
ihn	?	*vous*	you
nicht	not	*pas*	step
gesehen	?	*vu ?*	?

If your Russian wishes to reply, hand him a Russian-Esperanto vocabulary, pointing to the following paragraph on the outside :

" To express anything by means of this vocabulary, in the international language, look for the words required in the vocabulary itself ; and for the terminations necessary to distinguish the grammatical forms, look in the grammatical appendix, under the respective headings of the parts of speech which you desire to express."

The whole of the grammatical structure is explained in a few lines in this appendix, so the grammar can be looked out as easily as the root words.

PART IV

SPECIMENS OF ESPERANTO, WITH GRAMMAR AND VOCABULARY

NOTE

THE best way of learning Esperanto is to begin at once to read the language. Do not trouble to learn the grammar and list of suffixes by themselves first. All this can be picked up easily in the course of reading.

In the following specimens the first two pieces are marked for beginners. Each part of a word marked off by hyphens is to be looked out separately in the vocabulary. By the time the beginner has read these two pieces carefully in this way he will know the grammar, and have a fair idea of the structure of the language and the use of affixes.

In order to save time in looking out words, and so quicken the process of learning, the English translation of the third piece is given in parallel columns. Therefore in this piece only the principal words, which might be unfamiliar to English readers, are given in the vocabulary. Word-formation and some points of grammar are explained in the notes.

To get a practical grasp of Esperanto, cover the left-hand (Esperanto) column with a piece of paper after reading it, and re-translate the English into Esperanto, using the notes. After half an hour per day of such exercise for two or three weeks, an ordinary educated person will know Esperanto pretty well.

N.B.—It is very important to acquire a correct pronunciation at the start. Study the pronunciation rules, and practise reading aloud before beginning to translate. *Read slowly.*

I

PRONUNCIATION

Vowels

THERE are no long and short, open and closed, vowels : just five simple, full-sounding vowels, always pronounced the same. English people must be particularly careful to make them sufficiently full.

a as *a* in Engl. "father."
e „ *ey* „   „   "they."
i „ *ee* „   „   "eel."
o „ *o* „   „   "hole," inclining to *o* in Engl. "more." (English speakers find it hard to pronounce a true *o*.)
u „ *oo* „   „   "moon."

In short, the vowels are as in Italian.

Diphthongs

aj as *eye* in Engl. "eye."
oj „ *oy* „   „   "boy."
aŭ „ *ow* „   „   "cow."
(*eŭ* „ *e...w* „   „   "get *w*et" : this sound does not often occur.)

Consonants

These are pronounced as in English, except the following :

c as *ts* in Engl. "bits."
ĉ „ *ch* „   „   "church."
g „ *g* „   „   "give."
ĝ „ *g* „   „   "gentle."
ħ „ *ch* „ Scotch "loch," or German "ich."
j „ *y* „ Engl. "yes."
ĵ „ *s* „   „   "pleasure."
ŝ „ *sh* „   „   "shilling."
ŭ „ *w* „   „   "cow" (only occurs in the diphthongs *aŭ* and *eŭ*).

Accent

Always upon the last syllable but one.

Example

The first few lines of piece 1 in the following specimens may be thus figured for English readers:

Gayseenyóroy—mee noon déeros ahl vee káylkine vórtoyn Ayspayráhntay. Mee kraydahs kay vee ówdos, kay Ayspayráhnto áystahs tray fahtséelah ki baylsónah léengvo.

N.B.—The precise sound of *e* is between *a* in "b*a*le" and *e* in "b*e*ll."

II

SPECIMENS OF ESPERANTO

1. PAROL-AD-O

GE-SINJOR-O-J—mi nun dir-os al vi kelk-a-j-n vort-o-j-n Esperant-e. Mi kred-as ke vi aŭd-os, ke Esperant-o est-as tre facil-a kaj bel-son-a lingv-o. Ver-e, ĝi est-as tiel facil-a, sonor-a kaj simpl-a, ke oni tut-e ne hav-as mal-facil-ec-o-n por lern-i ĝi-n. La lern-ant-o-j pov-as ordinar-e kompren-i, leg-i, skrib-i kaj parol-i ĝin en tre mal-long-a temp-o. La fakt-o ke Esperant-o en-hav-as tre mal-mult-a-j-n, vokal-a-j-n son-o-j-n, kaj ke la vokal-o-j est-as ĉiu-j long-a-j kaj plen-son-a-j, est-ig-as ĝin mult-e pli facil-a ol la ali-a-j lingv-o-j, ĉu por aŭd-i, ĉu por el-parol-i.

Mi kred-as ke mal-long-a lern-ad-o est-os sufiĉ-a por vi-n kompren-ig-i, ke la hom-o-j de ĉiu-j naci-o-j pov-as inter-parol-i Esperant-e sen mal-facil-ec-o.

Mi ne de-ten-os vi-n pli long-e. Fin-ant-e, mi las-os kun vi du fraz-et-o-j-n: unu-e, por la ideal-ist-o-j, kiu-j cel-as unu frat-ec-o-n inter la popol-o-j de ĉiu land-o, la Esperant-a-n deviz-o-n—"Dum ni spir-as ni esper-as": du-e, por la hom-o-j praktik-a-j la praktik-a-n konsil-o-n—"Lern-u Esperant-o-n."

2. La Mar-bord-ist-o-j : Alegori-et-o

Ĉirkaŭ grand-a mez-ter-a mar-o viv-is mult-a-j popol-o-j. Ili hav-is mult-a-n inter-a-n komerc-o-n. Ĉar la mar-o est-is oft-e mal-trankvil-a kaj ili hav-is nur mal-grand-a-j-n ŝip-o-j-n, ili vetur-is laŭ-long-e la mar-bord-o, neniam perd-ant-e la ter-o-n el la vid-o.

Cert-a hom-o el-pens-is ŝip-o-n, kiu ir-is per vapor-o. Li dir-is al la mar-bord-ist-o-j : "Jen, ni met-u ni-a-n mon-o-n kun-e, kaj ni konstru-u grand-a-j-n vapor-ŝip-o-j-n. Tiel ni vetur-os rekt-e trans la mar-o unu al ali-a-n ; kaj ni far-os pli da komerc-o en mal-pli da temp-o." Sed la mar-bord-ist-o-j pli-am-is ĉirkaŭ-ir-i en mal-grand-a-j ŝip-o-j, kiel ili kutim-is. La el-pens-int-o ne hav-is sufiĉ-e da mon-o por konstru-i grand-a-n vapor-ŝip-o-n, kiu tre mult-e en-hav-os kaj tre rapid-e vojaĝ-os ; tial li dev-is vetur-ad-i en si-a mez-grand-a vapor-ŝip-o, kiu tamen almenaŭ rekt-e ir-is ĉie-n. Sed la mar-bord-ist-o-j daŭr-ig-is rem-i kaj vel-i ĉirkaŭ-e.

3. Nesaĝa Gento : Alegorio	An Unwise[1] Race : an Allegory
Malproksime, en nekonata lando, vivis sovaĝa gento. Ili loĝis en la mezo de vasta ebenaĵo, izolata de la ekstera mondo. Unuflanken homo dek tagojn	Far[2] away, in an unknown[3] land, there lived a savage race. They dwelt in the midst of a vast plain,[4] cut off from the outer[5] world. Towards one side[6] a man

---

[1] Unwise. Wise = *saĝa* ; *ne* = not.

[2] Far. Near = *proksim-e* (*e* = adverbial ending). To be near = *proksimi*. *Mal-* is a prefix denoting the opposite.

[3] Unknown. To know = *koni*. Pres. part. pass. *-at-*. Negative = *ne*. (*bona* = good ; *malbona* = bad ; *nebona* = not good.)

[4] Plain. Flat = *eben-a*. *aj* is a suffix denoting something made from or possessing the quality of.

[5] Outer. Outside (preposition) = *ekster*. *a* denotes an adjective.

[6] Towards one side. Side = *flank-o*. *e* denotes an adverb ; *flanke* = "sidely," i.e. at the side. *n* denotes motion towards.

vojaĝante venus al montegaro : aliflanke staris granda lago kaj senlimaj marĉoj. Tiel oni vivadis trankvile laŭ patra kutimo, tute senzorga pri la ago kaj faro de aliaj homgentoj transmontanaj. En somero estis varmege, kaj ĉiu vintro ŝajnis pli malvarma ol la antaŭa ; sed la tero estis fruktodona, ĝi donis al ili sufiĉe da greno por manĝi, kaj la riveroj kaj riveretoj plene provizis puran trinkaĵon.

Tiel ili vivadis ne malfeliĉe, kaj ilia vivo estis la vivo de la prapatroj, ĉar ili ne sciis kiel ĝin plibonigi. Sed man-

journeying [1] ten days [2] would come to a big mountain-range [3] ; on the other side stood a great lake and boundless [4] swamps. Thus [5] they lived [6] quietly after the manner of their fathers, caring nothing [7] for the way of life [8] of other men beyond the hills. In summer it was very hot, [9] and every winter seemed colder than the last ; but the earth was fertile, it gave them enough corn [10] to eat, and the streams and rivers furnished abundance of pure water to drink. [11]

Thus they lived not unhappily, and their life was the life of their forefathers, for they knew not how to better [12] it. But in their

[1] Journeying. This participial phrase qualifies the verb, *venus*, like an adverb. In Esperanto the participle therefore takes an *e*, which denotes an adverb.

[2] Ten days, i.e. for the duration of ten days. Duration of time is put in the accusative case.

[3] Big mountain-range. Mountain = *mont-o*. *eg* is a suffix denoting bigness ; *ar* is a suffix denoting a collection.

[4] Boundless. Limit = *lim-o*. Without = *sen*.

[5] Thus. See p. 193 for correlatives.

[6] They lived. To live = *viv-i*. *ad* is a suffix denoting continued action.

[7] Caring nothing. Care = *zorg-o*. Sen = without. *a* denotes an adjective.

[8] Way of life. Lit. the acting and doing.

[9] It was very hot. In such impersonal uses of the adjective, the adverbial form is used.

[10] Enough corn. *da* is used after words of quantity. *Sufiĉan grenon* would also be right.

[11] Water to drink. Lit. drink-stuff, or drink-thing.

[12] Better. Good = *bon-a* ; better = *pli bona* ; suf. *-ig* is causative.

kis en ilia lando unu aĵo, kaj pro tiu ĉi manko ili multe suferis : en la tuta lando ĉeestis nenia ŝirmilo, ĉu kontraŭ la suno en somero, ĉu por forteni la vintrajn ventojn. Ĉiuflanke la tero estis plata ; kaj kvankam la greno kaj ĉiuspecaj legomoj kreskis bone, arboj estis nekonataj. Eĉ la malproksima montaro staris tutnuda ; kaj kiam la ventoj blovis forte el ĝiaj neĝoj, la mizeruloj tremetis pro malvarmeco, kaj ne povis eĉ en siaj dometoj komfortiĝi, ĉar la penetranta enfluo de malvarma aero ŝtele eniris ĝis la familian kamenon.

Nu okazis ke certa knabo, pensema preter siaj jaroj,

land one thing[1] was lacking, and for[2] lack of this they suffered greatly : there was[3] no shelter[4] in all the land, whether against the sun in summer, or to keep off[5] the winter winds. On every side the ground was flat ; and although corn and all kinds of[6] vegetables grew well, trees were unknown. Even the distant mountains stood all bare ; and when the winds blew strong from amidst their[7] snows, the poor folk shivered for cold, and could not get comfortable[8] even in their cottages, for the penetrating draught of the cold air crept[9] right in to the family fireside.

Now, it happened that a certain boy, thoughtful[10] beyond his years,

---

[1] One thing. The concrete suffix -aĵ by itself may be used to express "thing." Of course it takes the substantival ending o.

[2] For lack. Esperanto is absolutely precise in the use of prepositions according to sense. No idiom. In this it differs from all other languages. Here " for " means " by reason of."

[3] There was. *Est-i* = to be ; *ĉe* = at ; *ĉeesti* = to be present.

[4] Shelter. To shelter = *ŝirm-i* ; *il* is a suffix expressing instrument.

[5] Keep off. To hold = *ten-i* ; away = *for*.

[6] All kinds of. Kind = *spec-o* ; all = *ĉiu*. *a* is adjectival ending.

[7] Their snows. Whose snows? The mountains'. Therefore *ĝiaj*, referring to *montaro*. If " their " referred to " winds," it would be *siaj*.

[8] Get comfortable. Comfort(able) = *komfort-o* (*a*) ; suf. *iĝ* denotes becoming.

[9] Crept in. To steal = *ŝtel-i* ; *-e* makes it an adverb.

[10] Thoughtful. To think = *pens-i* ; suf. *-em* denotes propensity.

komencis pripensi tiun ĉi mizeran staton. Li vivis kun sia vidvina patrino, kiu havis du infanetojn krom Namezo (tiel nomiĝis la knabo). Ili estis tre malriĉaj, kaj devis senĉese labori por nutri sin mem kaj la infanojn. La vidvino ne havis pli ol kvardek jarojn, sed Namezo rimarkis ke vespere, post la taga laboro, ŝi ŝajnis tute lacega, kaj kelkajn jarojn post la morto de sia edzo ŝi ekmaljuniĝis. Ofte la knabo diris al ŝi, ke ŝi devus pli ripozi, sed ĉiumatene post la nokto ŝi havis mienon tiel same lacegan kiel vespere; kaj ŝi plendis ke la trablovaj ventoj suferigis ŝin nokte per reŭmatismaj doloroj, kaj somere ŝi ne povis dormi pro varmeco. Tiam la knabo turnis la okulojn ekster sia

began to think over this wretched state of things. He lived with his[1] widowed mother, who had two little children besides Namezo (this was the lad's name[2]). They were very poor, and were obliged to work hard without stopping to get food for themselves and the children. The widow was not more than forty, but Namezo noticed that of an evening, after the day's work, she seemed quite tired out,[3] and a few years[4] after her husband's death she grew old all at once.[5] Often the boy told her she ought to take more rest, but every morning[6] she had the same worn-out look as in the evening; and she complained that the winds blowing through of a night plagued[7] her with[8] rheumatic pains, and in summer she could not sleep because of the heat. Then the boy turned

---

[1] With his widowed mother, i.e. his own = *sia*.

[2] This was his name. To name = *nom-i* ; with suf. -*iĝ* = to get named, to be called.

[3] Tired out. Tired = *lac-a* ; suf. -*eg* denotes intensity.

[4] A few years. Accusative of time.

[5] She grew old all at once. Young = *jun-a* ; old = *maljuna* ; suf. -*iĝ* denotes becoming ; prefix *ek-* denotes beginning, or sudden action.

[6] Every morning = *ĉiumatene*. "The whole morning" would be *la tutan matenon*.

[7] Plagued. To suffer = *sufer-i* ; suf. -*ig* is causative ; *suferigi* = to cause to suffer.

[8] With . . . pains. Think of the sense. "With" = by means of.

hejmo kaj rigardis ĉirkaŭen. Li vidis ke ĉiuflanke estis tiel same : la geviroj frue maljuniĝis kaj multe suferis. Li pensis, "Baldaŭ estos al mi ankaŭ simile ; la juneco estas mallonga kaj labora, kaj la vivo estas longa kaj ĉagrena." Fine li malgajadis.

Vintro forpasis, somero alvenis. Unu nokton la knabo estis kuŝanta en sia lito : li estis laboreginta en la kampoj, kaj estis tre laca, sed ju pli li penis ekdormi, des pli li obstine vekiĝadis. La tutan fajran tagon la suno estis malsupren brilinta sur la tegmenton de la dometo, tiel ke la kuŝejo nun similis fornon. Namezo pensis kaj turniĝis, returniĝis kaj repensis ; la samaj pensoj, ĉiam ronde revenantaj, iĝis turmento. Fine li ekdormetis,

his eyes outwards from his home and looked around him. He saw that on every side it was the same [1] : men and women [2] grew old early and suffered much. He thought, "Soon it will be the same with me ; youth [3] is short and full of work, and life is long and full of trouble." At last he became gloomy altogether. [4]

Winter passed away, summer came on. One night the boy was lying in his bed : he had been working hard [5] in the fields, and was very tired, but the more he tried to go to sleep [6] the wider awake he grew. All through the long fiery day the sun had been beating down [7] on the roof of the cottage, so that the sleeping-place [8] was now like an oven. Namezo thought and tossed, tossed and thought again ; the same thoughts, always coming round in a circle, became [9] a

---

[1] It was the same. Impersonal: use the adverbial form in *-e*.

[2] Men and women. Pref. *ge-* denotes both sexes.

[3] Youth. Young = *jun-a* ; suf. *-ec* denotes abstract.

[4] Became gloomy altogether. Gay = *gaj-a* ; gloomy = *malgaja* ; suf. *-ad* denotes continuance.

[5] He had been working hard. Pluperfect, lit. he was having worked. Suf. *-eg* denotes intensity.

[6] To go to sleep. To sleep = *dorm-i* ; pref. *ek-* denotes beginning.

[7] Down. Above = *supr-e* ; below = *malsupre* ; *n* denotes motion.

[8] Sleeping-place. To lie = *kuŝ-i* ; suf. *-ej* denotes place.

[9] Became. Suf. *-iĝ* denotes becoming ; here used as a separate verb.

sed la konfuzigaj pensoj, ĉiam la pensoj, ruladis eĉ en lia dormo senkompate tra lia cerbo.

Subite ekfalis sur lin granda paco. Li ŝajnis stari sur monta pinto. Laceco kaj zorgo ne estis plu. Ĉirkaŭe vasta soleco. Li kaj la monto —krom tio ekzistis nenio, kaj li estis kontenta.

Al li, tiel lukse enspiranta la freŝan aeron, alvenis fluge blanka birdo. Ĝi aperis, li ne sciis kiel, el la ĉirkaŭanta soleco, kaj metiĝis apud li sur la montan pinton. Ĝi komencis paroli, kaj en lia songo tio ĉi neniel lin surprizis.

"Homa knabo," diris la

torture. At length he fell into a light sleep,[1] but the distracting[2] thoughts, always the thoughts, kept rolling[3] through his brain pitilessly, even in his sleep.

All at once a great peace fell upon him. He seemed to be standing on a mountain-peak. Weariness[4] and care were no more. Around vast solitude. He and the mountain—there was nought else, and he was glad.

While he thus breathed in the fresh air with delight, a white bird came flying.[5] It appeared, he knew not how, out of the surrounding solitude,[6] and came and perched[7] beside him on the mountain-top. It began to speak, and in his dream this[8] in no way[9] astonished him.

"Mortal[10] boy," said the bird,

[1] Fell into a light sleep. To sleep = *dorm-i* ; suf. *-et* denotes light sleep ; pref. *ek-* denotes beginning.

[2] Distracting. Confused = *konfuz-a* ; suf. *-ig* denotes causation, confusion-causing.

[3] Kept rolling. To roll = *rul-i* ; suf. *-ad* denotes continuance.

[4] Weariness. Tired = *lac-a* ; suf. *-ec* denotes abstract.

[5] Came flying. To fly = *flug-i* ; root *flug-* with adverbial ending *-e* = flyingly.

[6] Solitude. Alone = *sol-a* ; suf. *-ec* denotes abstract.

[7] Came and perched. The idea of motion is conveyed by the accusative (*-n*) *pinton*.

[8] This. Use neuter form in *-o*, because it stands alone. "This dream" = *tiu ĉi songo*.

[9] In no way. See table of correlatives, p. 193.

[10] Mortal. Man = *hom-o* ; ending *-a* makes it an adj.

birdo, faligante en lian manon semon el sia beko, "prenu tiun ĉi semon : metu ĝin en la teron : prizorgu ĝin, flegu ĝin, kaj flegadu ĝin. Post tempo plenigota leviĝos el tiu ĉi semo kreskaĵo tia, kian la viaj ĝis nun ne vidis. La aliaj homoj nomas ĝin *arbon*. Ĝi estos granda ; kaj en la venontaj jaroj, se oni deve ĝin flegos, naskiĝos el ĝi arbaroj, kiuj estos ŝirmilo por la homaro, kaj por multaj aliaj celoj utilos. Sed flegi ĝin oni devos, ĉar sen homa penado nenio al homoj prosperas."

Namezo volis respondi, sed dum li levis la manon por rigardi la semon, estis al li kvazaŭ li turniĝis, la kapo malsupren : la monto malaperis, kaj li falis . . . falis . . . falis. . . .

Tiam li estis denove veka en la forna dometo, sed li

dropping [1] a seed into his hand from its beak, "take this seed : put it in the ground : care for it, tend it, and keep tending it. In the fulness of time there will rise [2] from this seed such [4] a growth [3] as [4] your people [5] never yet saw. Other peoples call it a *tree*. It will be big ; and in future [6] years, if it is duly tended, there will spring from it groves,[7] which will give shelter to men and women, and will be useful for many other ends. But tended it must be, for without man's striving nothing turns out well for men."

Namezo was about to reply, but as he raised his hand to look at the seed, he seemed to turn [8] head downwards : the mountain disappeared,[9] and he fell . . . fell . . . fell. . . .

Then he was awake again in the oven-like [10] hut, but he could

---

[1] Dropping. To fall = *fal-i* ; suf. *-ig* denotes causing to fall.

[2] Rise. To raise = *lev-i* ; suf. *-iĝ* makes it intransitive.

[3] A growth. To grow = *kreski* ; "grow-thing" = *kresk-aĵ-o*.

[4] Such . . . as. *Tia . . . kia* (= Latin *talis . . . qualis*). See table of correlatives, p. 193.

[5] Your people. You = *vi* ; *-a* makes it an adj.

[6] Future. Future participle active of *ven-i* = about to come.

[7] Groves. Tree = *arb-o* ; suf. *-ar* denotes a collection of trees.

[8] To turn. *Turn-i* is transitive ; suf. *-iĝ* makes it intransitive.

[9] Disappeared. To appear = *aper-i* ; pref. *mal-* denotes opposite.

[10] Oven-like. Oven = *forn-o* ; ending *-a* makes it an adjective.

ne povis sin malhelpi, rigardi sian manon, por vidi ĉu la semo enestis. Semo neestis: kaj la pensoj rekomencis ruladi tra lia cerbo—tamen ne plu la antaŭaj turmentigaj pensoj, sed novaj esperplenaj pensoj, ĉar li kredis, pasie kredis, ke estas ja ia veraĵo en lia songo.

Kaj nun la morgaŭa tago eklumiĝis. Li leviĝis kaj iris al sia laboro, kaj tiun ĉi tagon kaj multajn sekvantajn tagojn li laboradis kiel kutime, parolante al neniu pri la sema songo.

Sed kiam la tempo de rikolto forpasis, li aĉetis dudektagan nutraĵon kaj donis al la patrino sian restan ŝparaĵon el la rikolta tempo (ĉar vi scias, ke en la sezono de rikolto bona laboristo gajnas pli ol

not refrain[1] from[2] looking at his hand, to see if the seed was in it. There was no seed; and the thoughts began to roll through his brain again—yet no longer the old[3] worrying thoughts, but new thoughts full of hope, for he believed, passionately believed, that there was indeed some truth[4] in his dream.

And now the new day began to dawn. He got up and went about his work, and this day and many succeeding days he went on working as usual, speaking to no one about his dream of the seed.

But when harvest-time was over, he bought food[5] enough for twenty days and gave his mother the rest[6] of his harvest-tide savings[7] (for you know that in the harvest season a good workman[8] earns more than at

---

[1] Refrain. To help = *help-i*; to hinder = *malhelpi*; to hinder himself = *malhelpi sin*.

[2] Refrain from looking. In Esperanto use the simplest construction possible, *as long as it is clear*. The simple infinitive *rigardi* is clear after *malhelpi sin*.

[3] The old thoughts. Before = *antaŭ*; ending -*a* makes it an adjective.

[4] Truth. Think of the sense. Here truth = " true-thing," so use suf. -*aĵ*. "Truth" = abstract virtue = *vereco*.

[5] Food. To feed = *nutr-i*; suf. -*aĵ* denotes stuff.

[6] The rest of. The rest = *rest-o*; ending -*a* makes it an adjective = remaining.

[7] Savings. To save up = *ŝpar-i*; *ŝpar-aĵ-o* = save-thing (i.e. sav*ed* thing).

[8] Workman. To work = *labor-i*; suf. -*ist* denotes the agent.

alitempe), dirante ke li devos vojaĝi, kaj forestos dudek tagojn. La patrino miregis, ĉar neniam antaŭe li estis lasinta ŝin eĉ unu tagon; sed li estis bona filo, kaj ŝi kontraŭstaris lin en nenio.

Li forvojaĝis do, kaj post kvin tagoj li ekvidis malproksime sur la horizonto blankan nubon, kiu dum la morgaŭa tago montriĝis kiel monta pinto. Namezo salutis ĝin, kaj de tiu momento, sen ia dubo, direktis sian iron tra la ebenaĵo ĉiam al ĝi.

Kiam li alvenis piedon de la montoj, la deka tago jam finiĝis. Efektive li estis grave trompiĝinta pri la distanco. Neniam antaŭe li vidis monton, kaj tial, kiam li ekvidis la pinton meze de la vojaĝo, li kredis ke li ĵus alvenas, kaj

other times), saying that he must[1] go on a journey, and would[1] be away for twenty days. His mother wondered greatly, for he had never left[2] her before even for a single day; but he was a good son to her, and she did not thwart him in anything.

So he journeyed forth, and in five days he began to see far off on the horizon a white cloud, which turned out[3] in the course of the next day to be a mountain-peak. Namezo saluted it, and from that moment, without any doubt, bent his course[4] across the plain constantly towards it.

When he came to the foot[5] of the mountains, the tenth[6] day was already drawing to an end. Indeed, Namezo had been greatly mistaken[7] in the distance. He had never seen a mountain before, and so, when he caught sight of the peak half-way, he thought he

---

[1] He *must* go . . . and *would* be away. Esperanto syntax is perfectly simple. Just use the tense which the speaker would use, here the future; or any tense, so long as the meaning is clear.

[2] He had left. Pluperfect = "he was having left," *esti* with past part. *active. Li estis lasita* would mean "he had been left."

[3] Turned out to be. To show = *montr-i*; with suf. *-iĝ*, *montriĝ-i* = to show itself, to become shown.

[4] His course. To go = *ir-i*; ending *-o* makes it a substantive = a going.

[5] To the foot. Motion; use the *-n* case.

[6] Tenth. Ten = *dek*; to form the ordinal numbers add *-a* to the cardinal.

[7] Mistaken. To deceive = *tromp-i*; suf. *-iĝ* makes it intransitive.

marŝis pli malrapide. Tri tagojn li pensis ĉiumatene, "Mi estos hodiaŭ vespere ĉe la montpiedo ; morgaŭ mi suprenrampos ĝis la pinton." Sed nun li sciis, ke li estas malfrua. Li formanĝis jam la duonon de sia provizaĵo, kaj dum la lastaj mejloj li ekvidis ke lia pinto estas parto de vasta senlima montegaro, ke ĝi ankoraŭ malproksimas kaj li tute ne tiel facile suprenros. Li kalkulis ke almenaŭ oktaga nutraĵo estos necesa por reiri hejmen de la piedo de la montaro, kaj tiom li tie enterigis por la returna vojaĝo. Sekve restis nur dutaga manĝaĵo por la suprena kaj malsuprena montiro.

Tre frue do li ekiris la dekunuan tagon, kaj penadis ĉiutage supren. Vespere li vidis ke li ankoraŭ havas plenan tagvojaĝon ĝis la pinton, kaj tiel li devos tre ŝpareme

was just getting there, and walked slower. For three days he thought every morning, "I shall be at the foot of the mountains this evening ; to-morrow I'll climb [1] to the top." But now he knew that he was late.[2] He had already eaten up half [3] of his provisions,[4] and for the last few miles he was beginning to see that his peak was part of a boundless mountain-range, that it was still far off and he would by no means get up so easily. He calculated that at least eight days' food would be needed to get home from the foot of the mountain-range, and he buried [5] that amount [6] there for the return journey. Thus only two days' provision was left for the ascent and descent of the mountain.

Very early, then, on the eleventh [7] day he set out, and toiled the whole day upwards. In the evening he saw that he still had a full day's journey to the top, and so he must be very

---

[1] Climb. *Supr-a, -e, -en* = upper, above, upwards.
[2] Late. Early = *fru-a* ; pref. *mal-* denotes opposite.
[3] Half. Two = *du* ; suf. *-on* denotes fractions. cf. *kvarono* = quarter.
[4] Provisions. Provide-stuff (i.e. provid*ed* stuff).
[5] Buried. Earth = *ter-o* ; in = *en* ; suf. *-ig* denotes causing to be.
[6] That amount. *Tiom*. See the table of correlatives, p. 193.
[7] Eleven = *dek-unu* ; add *-a* to make the ordinal. 20 = *dudek*.

uzi sian restan provizaĵon. La dekdua tago estis tre doloriga. La monto fariĝis kruta ; li devis rapidi ; kaj li terure malsatis pro ekmankanta manĝaĵo. Malgraŭ ĉio li alvenis montpinton je la noktiĝo. La subita ekscito, kune kun la laceco kaj malsato, estis tro : en la momento de sukceso li falis en sveno sur la teron.

Jen, dum li kuŝis senkonscie, aperis la duan fojon la sama vidaĵo. Birdo blanka alflugis, metis en lian manon semon, kaj diris la samajn vortojn. Denove li levis la manon, kaj denove li ŝajnis renversiĝi, kaj falis . . . falis . . . falis. . . .

Rekonsciiĝinte, li trovis sin kuŝanta trankvile apud la loko mem, kie li enterigis sian returnan provizaĵon antaŭ la supreniro. Li kuŝis sur dolĉa

sparing [1] in the use of his remaining stores. The twelfth day was very painful.[2] The mountain grew [3] steep ; he had to press on ; and he was terribly hungry,[4] as the food was beginning to give out. In spite of all, he reached the top at nightfall.[5] The sudden excitement, with his weariness and hunger, was too much : in the moment of success he fell to the ground in a swoon.

And lo ! as he lay unconscious, there appeared to him for the second time the same vision.[6] A white bird flew up, put a seed into his hand, and said the same words. Again he raised his hand, and again he seemed to turn over, and fell . . . fell . . . fell. . . .

When he came to himself,[7] he was lying quietly in the very place where he had buried his food for the home journey before the ascent. He was lying

---

[1] Sparing. To save = ŝpar-i ; suf. -em denotes propensity.

[2] Painful. Pain = dolor-o ; suf. -ig denotes causation ; ending -a makes it an adjective.

[3] Grew. To make = far-i ; suf. -iĝ denotes becoming made, growing.

[4] Hungry. Satisfied = sat-a ; pref. mal- denotes the opposite. To be hungry = mal-sat-i.

[5] Nightfall. Night = nokt-o ; suf. -iĝ denotes becoming.

[6] Vision. See(n)-thing ; vid-i = to see ; with suffix -aĵ.

[7] When he came to himself. Conscious = konsci-a ; prefix re- denotes back again ; suffix -iĝ denotes becoming.

herbo, kaj sentis sin korpe tute mallacigata, kaj granda paco regis en lia animo. Tuj kiam li malfermis la okulojn, li rigardis en sian manon, kaj tiun ĉi fojon la semo enestis.

Longa, labora kaj preskaŭ sennutra malsupreniro de la montpinto jam ne necesis, kaj la hejmvojaĝo trans la ebenaĵo prosperis, tiel ke Namezo staris baldaŭ ree en la patrina dometo. La vilaĝanoj kunvenis amase kaj multe demandis pri lia vojaĝo, ĉar neniu el ili estis iam tiel malproksimen foririnta de la hejmo. Namezo ĉion rakontis, kaj montris la semon kiun li devos planti. La najbaroj komence kredis, ke li volas mirigi ilin, kiel la vojaĝistoj amas fari, kaj ili ridis pri liaj rakontaĵoj. Sed, kiam ili vidis ke li estis serioza, ili ekkoleriĝis kaj volis forpreni lian semon kaj detrui ĝin.

on soft grass, and his body felt free from its tiredness,[1] and in his soul reigned a great peace. As soon as he opened [2] his eyes, he looked in his hand, and this time the seed was there.

A long, laborious descent from the mountain-top almost without food was now no longer needful, and on the home journey across the plain all went well, so that Namezo soon stood again in his mother's [3] cottage. The villagers flocked in crowds [4] and asked many questions about his journey, for none of them had ever been so far from home. Namezo told them everything, and showed the seed which he was to plant. At first the neighbours thought he was trying to astonish [5] them, as travellers are wont to do, and they laughed at his tales. But when they saw that he was in earnest, they got in a rage,[6] and wanted to take away his seed and destroy it. " A ' tree ' is foolish-

---

[1] Free from tiredness. Tired = *lac-a* ; *mal-* denotes opposite ; *-ig* denotes causing to be.

[2] Opened. To shut = *ferm-i* ; to open = *malfermi*.

[3] Mother's. Father = *patr-o* ; suf. *-in* denotes feminine ; ending *-a* makes it an adjective.

[4] In crowds. Crowd = *amas-o* ; ending *-e* makes it an adverb.

[5] Astonish. To wonder = *mir-i* ; suf. *-ig* makes it transitive.

[6] Got in a rage. Anger = *koler-o* ; pref. *ek-* denotes beginning ; suf. *-iĝ* denotes becoming.

" 'Arbo' estas sensencaĵo,"
ili diris ; " ne povas ekzisti
alia kreskaĵo, krom la rikoltoj
kaj la legomoj kiujn ni kaj
niaj patroj jam ĉiam kreskigis.
Estas neeble ke io alia kresku
kaj iĝu pli granda." Kaj
unuj diris ke li estas vana
sonĝisto, kaj aliaj ke li
frenezas. Sed lia patrino
kuraĝigis lin.

Kaj Namezo timis por sia
semo, kaj pripensis kiel li
povos savi ĝin de la najbaroj
kiam ĝi ekkreskos. Kaj li
eliris el la vilaĝo nokte, kaj
plantis ĝin malproksime de
ĉiuj domoj, apud rivereto en
malleviĝo de la tero, kie oni
ĝin ne vidos ĝis ĝi estos tre
granda. Kaj komence li iris
tien nur nokte ; sed, ĉar li ne
parolis plu pri sia semo, la
vilaĝanoj forgesis la aferon,
tiel ke li povis eliri el la vilaĝo
vespere post sia taglaboro
kiam li volis, kaj neniu zorgis
pri tio, kien li iras. Sed li ne
kuraĝis ĝin transplanti apud

ness," [1] they said ; " no other
plant can exist, except the crops
and vegetables that we and our
fathers have always grown. It is
impossible for anything else to
grow and become [2] bigger than
they." And some said that he
was an idle dreamer, and others
that he was mad. But his
mother encouraged him.

And Namezo feared for his
seed, and thought how he could
save it from the neighbours when
it began to grow up. And he
went out of the village by night,
and planted it far away from all
the houses, by a little stream in
a hollow [3] of the ground, where
it would not be seen till it grew
very big. And at first he went
there only by night ; but, as he
said no more about his seed, the
villagers forgot the matter, so
that he could go out of the
village in the evenings after his
day's work whenever he liked,
and nobody troubled about where
he was going.[4] But he did not

---

[1] Foolishness. Sense = *senc-o* ; without = *sen* ; suf. *-aĵ* = without-sense-stuff.

[2] Become. Suf. *-iĝ* is here used alone as a verb = to become.

[3] A hollow. To raise = *lev-i* ; suf. *-iĝ* makes it intransitive ; pref. *mal-*
denotes the opposite ; ending *-o* makes it a noun.

[4] Where he was going. "Where" here = "whither," therefore add *-n*,
which denotes motion.

sian dometon, timante ke oni difektu ĝin aŭ ŝerce aŭ malice, kaj sekve restis por li la granda laborado iri, kiam li estis jam laca, malproksimen por flegi ĝin.

Jaroj forpasadis : Namezo grandiĝis, sed lia kreskaĵo ne volis grandiĝi. Multfoje li malesperis, vidante ke ĝi kvazaŭ ne kreskadis plu, aŭ ke ĝi en somero havis velkan mienon. Multajn vintrojn ĝi preskaŭ mortis per frosto. Sed li persistis, kaj ĉiuokaze li provis ian novan flegon, ĉar neniam antaŭe en la tuta lando oni kreskigis tielan plantaĵon. Iatempe li metis sterkon : tiam li subdrenis la teron, ĉirkaŭhakis la branĉetojn, aŭ ŝirmis la burĝonojn kontraŭ la ventoj. Ree, vidante ke malgraŭ ĉio la arbeto ne prosperis, li pretigis novan teraĵon kaj transplantis ĝin, antaŭe enpluginte alispecan teron. Li eksperimentis per seka, poste per malseka, subtero : unu-

dare to transplant it to his own cottage, fearing that they would damage it in jest or malice, and so the hard work remained for him of going a long way to look after it, when he was already tired.

Years passed away : Namezo grew up,[1] but his plant would not grow up too. Many a time he despaired,[2] seeing that it seemed as though it had given up growing, or that it had a faded look in summer. Many winters it nearly died of the frosts. But he persevered, and in every case [3] he tried some new treatment, for never before in the whole land had any one grown [4] such a plant. At one time he would put on manure ; then he tried draining the ground, pruning the shoots, or protecting the buds against the winds. Again, seeing that in spite of all the little tree did not flourish, he prepared [5] a new soil-bed and transplanted it, having first ploughed in a different kind of earth. He experimented with dry, and then with damp, sub-soil :

---

[1] Grew up. Big = *grand-a* ; suf. *-iĝ* denotes becoming.

[2] Despaired. To hope = *esper-i* ; pref. *mal-* denotes opposite.

[3] In every case. To happen = *okaz-i* ; any or all = *ĉiu* ; ending *-e* makes it adverbial = "any-happening-ly," i.e. whatever happened.

[4] Grown. To grow (intrans.) = *kresk-i* ; suf. *-ig* makes it transitive.

[5] Prepared. Ready = *pret-a* ; suf. *-ig* = to make ready.

vorte, li senĉese penadis, diversigante konstante la kondiĉojn ĝis li ĝuste trafos. Fine, kiam li jam de longe estis plenaĝa, lia deziro plenumiĝis : tie, apud la rivereto staris granda belkreska *arbo*.

En somero, kiam la folioj estis plenaj, li kondukis tien kelkajn amikojn, kaj ili ĝojis sidantaj vespere sub la freŝa ombro. En aŭtuno ili kolektis la semujojn, portis ilin en la vilaĝon, kaj penis decidigi la vilaĝanojn planti la semaron apud siaj dometoj, por havi ŝirmilon. Sed la vilaĝanoj ne volis.

Unu diris, "Arbo estas neebla."*

Kaj Namezo respondis, "Arbo ekzistas. Venu kun mi, kaj mi vidigos vin."

Sed li diris, "Arbo estas neebla."

Ree Namezo diris, "Se vi

in short, he toiled ceaselessly, constantly varying[1] the conditions till he should hit off the right thing. At last, when he had long come to be a grown man,[2] his desire was fulfilled :[3] there beside the stream stood a fine big *tree*.

In summer, when it was in full leaf, he took his friends there, and they rejoiced sitting in the cool shade at evening. In autumn they collected the pods,[4] took them to the village, and tried to get the villagers to plant the seed by their homes, to give them shelter. But the villagers would not have them.

One said, "A tree is impossible."[5]

And Namezo answered, "A tree exists. Come with me, and I will show[6] you."

But he said, "A tree is impossible."

Again Namezo said, "If you

---

[1] Varying. Diverse = *divers-a* ; suf. -*ig* = to render diverse.

[2] A grown man. Age = *aĝ-o* ; full = *plen-a* ; ending -*a* denotes adj.

[3] Was fulfilled. To fulfil = *plenum-i* ; -*iĝ* denotes becoming.

[4] Pods. Seed = *sem-o* ; suf. -*uj* denotes that which contains.

[5] Impossible. Suf. -*ebl* denotes possibility, and can, like all suffixes, be used by itself. *Ne-ebl-a* = not possible.

[6] Show. To see = *vid-i* ; with suf. -*ig* = to cause to see.

* For this and the following objections of the villagers, compare Part I., chap. xv., pp. 54-6.

nur tiom da peno faros, kiom necesas por eliri el la vilaĝo, mi montros al vi arbon, sub kiu miaj amikoj kaj mi ŝirmiĝas ĉiuvespere. Venu nur kaj provu se ĝi plaĉos ankaŭ al vi."

Sed li diris, "Mi ne volas eliri. Arbo estas neebla."

Alia diris, "Mi vidis vian arbon, kaj mi trovas ĝin tute senutila."

Kaj Namezo respondis, "Kial?"

Kaj li diris, "Niaj patroj ne havis arbon."

Namezo diris, "Niaj patroj suferis pro manko de ŝirmado."

Kaj li diris, "Tial mi ankaŭ suferos."

Alia diris, "Ni havas ja sufiĉe da kreskaĵoj. Niaj rikoltoj kaj legomoj provizas nutraĵon, kaj la belaj floroj ĉarmas la okulon. Alia kreskaĵo estus superflua."

Kaj Namezo respondis, "Bone. Niaj ĝisnunaj kreskaĵoj plenumas la ĉefajn bezonojn de la homaro. Manĝo kaj certa ornamo estas necesaĵoj por la homa naturo, kaj

will only take as much trouble [1] as is necessary to go out of the village, I will show you a tree, under which my friends and I take shelter every evening. Only just come and try whether it pleases you also."

But he said, "I will not go out. A tree is impossible."

Another said, "I have seen your tree, and I consider it perfectly useless."

And Namezo answered, "Why?"

And he said, "Our fathers had no trees."

Namezo said, "Our fathers suffered from want of shelter."

And he said, "Therefore I too will suffer."

Another said, "We have enough plants. Our crops and vegetables provide food, and our gay flowers charm the eye. Another growing thing would be superfluous."

And Namezo answered, "Good. The plants we have already [2] fulfil the chief needs of mankind. Food and some ornament are necessities [3] for human nature, and for these uses we have the

---

[1] Trouble. To try = *pen-i*; ending *-o* makes it a substantive = trying, effort.

[2] The plants we have already. Lit. our till-now plants.

[3] Necessities. Necessary = *neces-a*; with suf. *-aĵ* = necessary things.

por tiuj ĉi uzoj ni havas rikoltojn kaj florojn. Sed la
vivo estus pli plezura se ni
estus pli bone ŝirmataj. Tiun
ĉi apartan servon prezentas la
arboj, kaj ni povos ĝui ĝin sen
fordoni la profiton de floro kaj
rikolto. Ne, plue, niaj rikoltoj,
ŝirmataj de la montaj ventoj,
pli facile maturiĝos: tiel ni
havos pli da tempo por la
plezurigaj laboroj, kaj la floroj
estus ankoraŭ pli belaj."

Kaj li diris, "Tagmeze,
kiam la suno brilas, mi kuŝas
inter la altstaranta greno. Tiu
ĉi ŝirmilo sufiĉas. Ni havas
sufiĉe da kreskaĵoj. Arbo
ne estas kreskaĵo; ĝi estas
monstro. Iru diablon!"

Kaj Namezo iris al la diablo,
ĉar li estis preta iri kien ajn,
plivole ol daŭrigi paroli kun
la vilaĝanoj.

Li diris, "Via diabla Moŝto,
la vilaĝanoj naŭzadas min,
kaj mi estas laca je mia vivo.
Faru el mi kion vi volas."

crops and flowers. But life would
be pleasanter if we were better
sheltered. This special service [1]
is done by the trees, and we can
enjoy it without foregoing the
advantage of flower and crop.
Nay, more, our crops, sheltered
from the winds that blow from
the mountains, will ripen [2] more
easily: thus we shall have more
time for the work that brings
pleasure, [3] and the flowers will
be even more lovely."

And he said, "At noon, [4] when
the sun shines warm, I lie amidst
the deep standing corn. This
shelter is enough. We have
plants enough. A tree is not a
plant; it is a monster. Go to
the devil!"

And Namezo went to the devil,
for he was ready to go anywhere,
rather than continue to talk to
the villagers.

He said, "Your devilish Majesty,
the villagers make me sick, [5] and
I am tired of [6] my life. Do with
me as you will."

---

[1] Service. To serve = serv-i; ending -o makes it a substantive.

[2] Ripen. Ripe = matur-a; suf. -iĝ denotes becoming.

[3] Work that brings pleasure. Pleasure = plezur-o; suf. -ig denotes causing
to be.

[4] Noon. Day = tag-o; middle = mez-o; ending -e is adverbial.

[5] Make me sick. To make sick = naŭz-i; -ad denotes continuation.

[6] Tired of. The preposition je is used when no other preposition exactly fits.

Respondis la diablo, "Mi ne povas ion fari por vi, mizerulo! La vilaĝanoj estas venkintaj min; kaj mi retiras min de la aferoj. Neniam, eĉ en miaj plej eltrovemaj tagoj, mi elpensis tiel mortigan turmenton por progresema homo, kiel sukcesi en la produkto de profitiga uzilo, kaj tiam devi penadi, por igi siajn kunulojn alpreni ĝin. Reiru al la vilaĝanoj kaj donu al ili miajn respektplenajn komplimentojn."

Pezakore, Namezo reiris hejmen, kaj envoje li renkontis vilaĝanaron portantan hakilojn. Li demandis kial ili portas hakilojn.

"Por dehaki la arbon," respondis la grupestro; "ni timas ke ĝi etendiĝos sur la tutan landon. Se oni prenos la fruktetojn kaj plantos ilin apud sia loĝejo, la arboj en-

The devil made answer, "I can do nothing for you, poor wretch![1] The villagers have beaten me; and I am retiring from business. Never, even in my most ingenious[2] days, did I invent such a deadly[3] torment for a progressive man, as to succeed in producing a beneficial[4] device, and then have to keep striving to get his fellows[5] to adopt it. Go back again to the villagers, and give them my respectful compliments."

Heavy at heart, Namezo went home again, and on the way he fell in with a band of villagers[6] carrying axes.[7] He asked why they were carrying axes.

"To cut down the tree," replied the leader of the band[8]; "we are afraid that it will spread and fill the whole land. If the people take the fruits and plant them at their own homes,[9] trees will

---

[1] Wretch. Misery = *mizer-o*; suf. *-ul* denotes having the quality of.
[2] Ingenious. To find = *trov-i*; out = *el*; suf. *-em* denotes propensity or aptitude.
[3] Deadly. To die = *mort-i*; suf. *-ig* denotes to cause to die.
[4] Beneficial. Profit-causing; suf. *-ig*.
[5] Fellows. With = *kun*; suf. *-ul* denotes state or quality.
[6] A band of villagers. Suf. *-ar* denotes a collection.
[7] Axes. To hew = *hak-i*; suf. *-il* denotes instrument.
[8] Leader of the band. Band = *grup-o*; suf. *-estr* denotes chief of.
[9] Homes. To dwell = *loĝ-i*; suf. *-ej* denotes place.

trudos sin en la kampojn kaj en la florbedojn, kaj elpuŝos la aliajn kreskaĵojn."

"Sed vi tute ne devos planti la arbojn en la kampoj kaj florbedoj," diris Namezo. La arboj havas utilon diferencan de la aliaj kreskaĵoj kaj oni plantos ilin en aparta loko. Se okaze arbo altrudos sin inter la rikoltojn, oni elradikos ĝin tuj, antaŭ ol ĝi grandiĝos."

"Ne, arbo estas danĝera," kriis la hakilistoj ; kaj Namezo devis alvoki siajn amikojn por defendi la arbon.

Poste Namezo iris hejmen kaj enfermis sin en sia dometo. Lia patrino estis jam de longe morta, kaj la gefratoj jam edziĝis, kaj li vivadis sole. Sed li nun ne povis eĉ resti sola. Venis la saĝuloj de la vilaĝo, kaj ili kriadis tra la fenestro, "Arbo estas bona ideo, sed vi kreskigis vian arbon malprave. Lasu nin do flegi ĝin laŭ nia bontrovo, kaj ni baldaŭ plibonigos ĝin,

encroach upon the fields and upon the flower-beds, and will drive out the other plants."

"But you must not plant the trees in the fields and flower-beds," said Namezo. "Trees have a different use from other plants, and they will be planted in quite separate places. If by chance a tree pushes itself in amongst the crops, it will be rooted out at once, before it gets big."

"No, trees are dangerous," cried the men with the axes [1] ; and Namezo had to call up his friends to defend the tree.

After this Namezo went home and shut himself up in his cottage. His mother was by this time long dead, and his brother and sister [2] were now married, [3] and he lived all alone. But now he could not even remain alone. The wise men of the village came along, and they kept shouting through the window, "Trees are a good idea, but you have grown your tree the wrong way. So let us look after it as we see fit, and we'll

[1] The men with the axes. To hew = *hak-i* ; *-il* denotes instrument ; *-ist* denotes agent.

[2] Brother and sister. Prefix *ge-* denotes both sexes.

[3] Were married. Husband (wife) = *edz* (*in*) *-o* ; suffix *-iĝ* denotes becoming.

tiel ke ĝi estos vere alpreninda arbo."

Kaj al ili Namezo respondis nenion. Li sciis ke li estis doninta grandan parton de sia vivo por eksperimenti kaj estis produktinta belkreskan arbon, dum la lertuloj nun estis vidantaj arbon je la unua fojo, kaj tute malsciis la malfacilecojn kiujn oni devas venki, kaj eĉ ne komprenis la demandon kiun ili entreprenis solvi. Sed li sciis ankaŭ ke tiela konsidero estas por lertuloj malpli ol nenio. Estis malutile argumenti kun ili, ĉar ili ne sciis ke ili ne scias, kaj tio ĉi estas plej malfacila lerni. Tial li lasis ilin paroladi, kaj flegis sian arbon kiel antaŭe. "Ĉar," li diris al si mem, "kiam la arbo estos disvastiĝinta kaj multobliĝinta laŭspece tra la lando, per la grada sperto de multaj homoj fariĝos arba scienco, kaj tial ni fine ellernos la plej bonan flegmanieron." Ankaŭ li pensis, "La diablo estis prava : la diablo estas lertulo."

Iom poste alvenis en la

soon improve[1] it, so that it shall be a tree really fit for us to take to."[2]

And to these Namezo answered nothing. He knew that he had given a great part of his life to making experiment and had produced a well-grown tree, while the clever men were now seeing a tree for the first time, and were wholly ignorant of the difficulties that had to be overcome, and did not even understand the question they were undertaking to solve. But he also knew that to clever men such a consideration is less than nothing. It was no good to argue with them, for they did not know that they did not know, and this is the hardest thing to learn. So he let them keep on talking, and tended his tree as before. "For," said he to himself, "when the tree has spread and multiplied after its kind throughout the land, from many men's gradual experience there will arise a science of trees, and thus we shall in the end find out the best way of tending them." Also he thought, "The devil was right : the devil is a clever man."

Now, some time after there

[1] Improve. Good = *bon-a* ; more = *pli* ; *-ig* denotes causation.
[2] Fit to take to. To take = *pren-i* ; to = *al* ; *-ind* denotes worthy.

vilaĝon homoj el aliaj lokoj, kunportantaj diversajn semojn. Ĉiu el ili laŭdis sian propran semon, dirante ke li estas kreskiginta belan arbon el tia semo, kaj postulante ke la vilaĝanoj plantu nur liajn semojn. Tiam iuj diris, " Ni metu ĉiujn la diversajn semojn kunen, kaj ni kreskigu el ili unu bonan arbon." Kaj tiuj ĉi petis Namezon ke li neniigu sian arbon kaj pistu ĝiajn semojn kaj almiksu ilin en la kunmetatan semaĵon, por ke unu bona arbo elkresku.

Tiel ili babiladis kaj bataladis inter si; kaj ili ĉirkaŭiradis en la vilaĝo, montrante modelojn de siaj arboj kaj pruvante, ĉiu ke la sia estas la plej bona. Kaj fine la vilaĝanoj enuiĝis kaj denove volis dehaki ĉiun kaj ĉies arbon.

Sed Namezo kaj liaj amikoj havis jam du aŭ tre grandajn arbojn, kaj ĝis nun prosperis al ili defendi ilin kontraŭ la atakoj de la vilaĝanoj. Kaj ĉiam, kiam la vetero estas varmega, ili sidas sub la arboj

arrived in the village men from other places, bringing with them various seeds. Each of them praised his own seed, telling how he had grown a fine tree from such seed, and urging the villagers to plant his seeds only. Then certain of them said, " Let us put all the divers seeds together, and let us grow from them one good tree." And these begged Namezo to destroy[1] his own tree and pound its seeds and stir them into the compound seedstuff, that one good tree might grow out of it.

Thus they babbled and kept quarrelling among themselves; and they went round about in the village showing models of their trees and proving each that his own was the best. And at last the villagers grew weary of it, and wanted again to hew down every tree, no matter to whom it belonged.[2]

But Namezo and his friends had by this time two or three big trees, and up to this day they have succeeded in defending them against the villagers' attacks. And always, when the weather is very hot, they sit under their trees

---

[1] Destroy. Nothing = *neni-o*; suf.-*ig* denotes causation.
[2] No matter to whom it belonged. Lit. every one's.

vespere kaj ĝuas la freŝecon. Tamen ili havas nur duonan profiton el ili, ĉar la vilaĝanoj malpermesas planti ian arbon en la vilaĝo, kaj tial la arbanoj devas ĉiufoje marŝi malproksimen kaj aparte viziti siajn arbojn, anstataŭ havi ilin apud siaj pordoj.

in the evening and enjoy the coolness. Yet have they only half profit by them, for the villagers forbid them to plant any tree in the village, and so the tree people have to walk a long way each time and have to make special visits to their trees, instead of having them at their doors.

Kaj la plej granda parto de la vilaĝanoj, malgraŭ ke oni povas facile piediri al la arboj, diras ankoraŭ, "Arbo estas neebla."

And the greater part of the villagers, though the trees are within a walk, still say, "Trees are impossible."

Kaj la diablo ridas.

And the devil laughs.

III

GRAMMAR

1. THERE is one definite article, *la*, invariable. There is no indefinite article.

2. Nouns always end in -*o*. Ex. *patro* = father.

3. Adjectives always end in -*a*. Ex. *patra* = paternal.

4. The plural of nouns, adjectives, participles, and pronouns (except only the personal pronouns) ends in *j*. Ex. *patroj* = fathers; *bonaj patroj* = good fathers.

5. The accusative (objective) case always ends in -*n*. Ex. *Mi amas mian bonan patron* = I love my good father. *Ni amas niajn bonajn patrojn* = we love our good fathers.

6. Adverbs always end in -*e*. Ex. *bone* = well; *patre* = paternally. (There are a few non-derived adverbs without the ending -*e*, as *jam, ankaŭ, tiel, kiel*).

7. The personal pronouns are :

mi = I	*ŝi* = she	*ni* = we
vi = you	*ĝi* = it	*vi* = you
li = he	*oni* = one	*ili* = they

Also a reflexive pronoun, *si*, which always refers to the subject of its own clause.

All these pronouns form the accusative case by adding *-n*.

8. The verb has no separate ending for person or number.

The present ends in *-as*.   Ex. *mi amas* = I love.

The past ends in *-is*.   Ex. *vi amis* = you loved.

The future ends in *-os*.   Ex. *li amos* = he will love.

The conditional ends in *-us*.   Ex. *ni amus* = we should love.

The imperative ends in *-u*.   Ex. *amu* = love ! *ni amu* = let us love.   This form also serves for subjunctive.   Ex. *Dio ordonas ke ni amu unu la alian* = God commands us to love one another.

The infinitive ends in *-i*.   Ex. *ami* = to love.

There are three active participles.

The present participle active is formed by *-ant*.   Ex. *amanta* = loving ; *amanto* = a lover.

The past participle active is formed by *-int*.   Ex. *aminta* = having loved ; *la skribinto* = the author (lit. the man who has written).

The future participle active is formed by *-ont*.   Ex. *amonta* = being about to love.

There are three passive participles.

The present participle passive is formed by *-at*.   Ex. *amata* = being loved.

The past participle passive is formed by *-it*.   Ex. *amita* = having been loved.

The future participle passive is formed by *-ot*.   Ex. *amota* = being about to be loved.

All compound tenses, as well as the passive voice, are formed by the verb *esti* (to be) with a participle.   Compound tenses are employed only when the simple forms are inadequate.   Ex. *mi estas aminta* = I have loved (lit. I am having loved); *vi estis aminta* = you had loved (lit. you were having loved) ; *ili estas amataj* = they are loved ; *ŝi estas amita* = she has been loved ; *ni estis amitaj* = we had been loved ; *ili estos amintaj* = they will have loved ; *ŝi estus aminta* = she would have loved ; *mi estus amita* = I should have been loved.

IV

LIST OF AFFIXES

I. *Prefixes*

bo- denotes relation by marriage : *bopatro* = father-in-law.

dis- denotes dissemination, division : *dismeti* = to put apart, about, in pieces.

ek- denotes sudden action or beginning : *ekdormi* = to fall asleep ; *ekiri* = to start.

ge- denotes both sexes : *gepatroj* = parents ; *geviroj* = men and women.

mal- denotes the opposite : *bona* = good ; *malbona* = bad.

re- denotes back, again : *repagi* = to repay ; *rekomenci* = to begin again.

II. *Suffixes*

-ad denotes continuation : *penadi* = to keep striving, to make continued effort.

-aĵ denotes something concrete, made of the material, or possessing the qualities of the root to which it is attached : *bovo* = ox; *bovaĵo* = beef; *okazi* = to happen ; *okazaĵoj* = happenings, events. (For English speakers a good rule is to add " thing " or " stuff" to the English word ; *propra* = one's own, *propraĵo* = own-thing, property ; *vidindaĵoj* = see-worthy-things, notable sights.

N.B. : *-aĵ* added to transitive verbal stems generally has a passive sense : *tondi* = to clip, *tondaĵo* = clipped-thing, clippings ; whereas *tondilo* = clipping-thing, shears.)   See Zamenhof's explanation of -aĵ, *La Revuo*, Vol. I., No. 8 (April), pp. 374-5.

-an denotes an inhabitant, member, or partisan : *urbano* = a town-dweller ; *Kristano* = a Christian.

-ar denotes a collection : *vortaro* = a dictionary ; *arbaro* = a forest ; *homaro* = mankind.

-ĉj denotes masculine affectionate diminutives : *paĉjo* = daddy ; *Arĉjo* = Arthur.

-ebl denotes possibility : *kredebla* = credible.

-ec denotes abstract quality : *boneco* = goodness.

-eg denotes great size or intensity : *grandega* = enormous ; *varmega* = intensely hot.

-ej denotes place : *lernejo* = a learn-place, a school.

-em denotes propensity to : *lernema* = studious ; *kredema* = credulous.

-er denotes one out of many, or a unit of a mass : *sablero* = a grain of sand ; *fajrero* = a spark.

-estr denotes a chief or leader : *lernejestro* = a head master.

-et denotes diminution : *infaneto* = a little child ; *varmeta* = warmish.

-id denotes the young of, descendant of : *bovido* = a calf.

-ig denotes causation : *bonigi*, *plibonigi* = to make good, to improve ; *mortigi* = to kill ; *venigi* = to cause to come, to send for.

-iĝ denotes becoming, and has a passive signification : *saniĝi*, *resaniĝi* = to get well (again) ; *paliĝi* = to grow pale ; *troviĝi* = to be found, occur.

-il denotes an instrument : *razilo* = a razor.

-in denotes feminine : *patrino* = mother ; *bovino* = cow.

-ind denotes worthiness : *laŭdinda* = laudable, praiseworthy.

-ing denotes a holder : *kandelingo* = a candlestick ; *glavingo* = scabbard.

-ist denotes profession or occupation ; *maristo* = a sailor ; *bonfaristo* = a benefactor.

-nj denotes feminine affectionate diminutives : *Manjo* = Polly ; *patrinjo* (or *panjo*) = mamma.

-uj denotes containing or producing : *inkujo* = inkpot ; *Anglujo* = England.

-ul denotes characteristic : *timulo* = a coward : *avarulo* = a miser.

[The suffix *-aĉ* (not in the *Fundamento*) is coming into use as a pejorative (= Italian *-accio*) : *ridi* = to laugh ; *ridaĉi* = to grin, sneer.]

V

TABLE OF CORRELATIVE WORDS

	Demonstrative.	Relative and Interrogative.	Negative.	Universal.	Indefinite.
Person *	tiu that	kiu who, which	neniu no one	ĉiu every, all, every one	iu some, some one
Thing *	tio that (thing)	kio what, which	nenio nothing	ĉio everything	io something
Quality	tia that kind of a	kia what kind of a	nenia no, no kind of	ĉia each, every kind of	ia any, some kind of
Time	tiam then	kiam when	neniam never	ĉiam always	iam ever at some time
Place	tie there	kie where	nenie nowhere	ĉie everywhere	ie somewhere
Manner	tiel thus, so	kiel how	neniel in no way	ĉiel in every way	iel in some way, somehow
Motive	tial therefore	kial why	nenial for no reason	ĉial for all reasons	ial for some reason
Quantity	tiom so ⎱ much as ⎰ many	kiom how much how many	neniom none	ĉiom the whole amount	iom somewhat, a certain amount
Possession	ties of that	kies whose, of which	nenies nobody's	ĉies everybody's	ies somebody's

In the demonstrative column, to express "this" instead of "that," add ĉi.

---

   * *N.B.*—*Tiu, kiu*, etc., are used in agreement with a noun expressed, even when it does not represent a person.

   Ex. *Tiu libro, kiun mi legis* = that book which I read.

   Tiuj ĉi floroj = these flowers.

Tio, kio, etc., are used when there is no noun, so that they stand alone.

   Ex. *Tio estas vera* = that is true; *kion vi diris?* = what did you say? *Tio ĉi estas pli granda ol tio* = this is bigger than that.

   N.B.—In memorizing the above, it is well to remember that *t* = demonstrative, *k* = relative-interrogative, *ĉ* = distributive, *i* = indefinite, *nen* = negative.

VI

VOCABULARY

A

-*a*, termination of adjectives.
aĉet-i, to buy.
-*ad*, suffix denoting continued action.
aer-o, air.
ag-i, to act.
-*aĵ*, suffix denoting concrete substance.
ajn, (what)ever; *kiu ajn*, whoever.
al, to.
ali-a, other.
almenaŭ, at least.
alt-a, high.
am-i, to love.
amas-o, crowd, mass.
ankaŭ, also.
ankoraŭ, still.
anstataŭ, instead of.
-*ant*, present participle active.
antaŭ, before (time and place).
apart-a, special.
apud, at.
-*ar*, suffix denoting a collection.
arb-o, tree.
-*as*, ending of present tense.
aŭd-i, to hear.

B

baldaŭ, soon.
bed-o, flower-bed.

bel-a, fine, beautiful.
bezon-o, need.
blank-a, white.
bon-a, good.
bord-o, edge, shore.
bril-i, to shine.
burĝon-o, bud.

C

cel-o, object, aim.
cerb-o, brain.
cert-a, certain.

Ĉ

ĉagren-o, trouble.
ĉar, for, because.
ĉe, at.
ĉes-i, to cease.
ĉi, added to demonstrative *tiu*, expresses nearer connexion: *tiu* = that; *tiu ĉi* = this.
ĉiam, always.
ĉie, everywhere.
ĉirkaŭ, around.
ĉiu, all, each, every.
ĉu, interrogative particle.

D

da, used after words of quantity: Ex. *multe da vino*, much wine.
daŭr-i, to last, continue.
de, of, from, by (with passive).

des, comparative particle ; *ju . . . des*, the . . . the : Ex. *ju pli des plibone*, the more the better.

dev-i, to owe, to be obliged to.

deviz-o, device, motto.

difekt-i, to spoil.

dir-i, to say.

dom-o, house.

don-i, to give.

du, two.

dub-i, to doubt.

dum, whilst.

E

-e, ending of adverbs.

eben-a, flat, level.

-ebl, suffix denoting possibility.

-ec, suffix denoting abstract quality : *bon-ec-o*, goodness.

eĉ, even.

edz-(in)-o, husband (wife).

-eg, suffix denoting great size.

-ej, suffix denoting place.

ek-, prefix denoting beginning.

ekster, outside.

el, out of.

-em, suffix denoting propensity.

en, in.

entrepren-i, to undertake.

enu-i, to weary, bore.

esper-i, to hope.

Esperant-o, Esperanto.

est-i, to be.

-et, suffix denoting little.

etend-i, to stretch.

F

facil-a, easy.

fajr-o, fire.

fakt-o, fact.

far-i, to do.

fenestr-o, window.

ferm-i, to shut.

fil-o, son.

fin-o, end.

flank-o, side.

fleg-i, to tend.

flu-i, to flow.

flug-i, to fly.

foj-o, time ; *du fojoj*, twice.

foli-o, leaf.

for, away.

forn-o, oven.

frato, brother.

fraz-o, sentence.

frenez-o, madness.

fru-a, early.

frukt-o, fruit.

G

ge-, prefix denoting both sexes.

gent-o, race, tribe.

grand-a, big, great.

Ĝ

ĝi, it.

ĝis, until.

ĝoj-o, joy.

ĝu-i, to enjoy.

H

hav-i, to have.
hejm-o, home.
hodiaŭ, to-day.
hom-o, man (mortal; no distinction of sex).

I

-i, ending of infinitive.
ideal-o, ideal.
-ig, suffix denoting causation.
-iĝ, suffix denoting becoming.
-il, suffix denoting instrument.
ili, they.
-int, past participle active.
inter, between, among.
ir-i, to go.
-is, ending of past tense.
-ist, suffix denoting agent.
iu, some one.

J

-j, ending of plural.
jam, already.
jar-o, year.
jen, here is, here are (French *voici*).
ju, comparative particle. See *des*.
jun-a, young.

Ĵ

jus, just now.

K

kaj, and.
kamen-o, fireplace.
kamp-o, field.
kap-o, head.
ke, that (conjunction).
kelk-a, some.
kiam, when.
kiel, how, as.
kiu, who, which.
knab-o, boy.
komerc-o, commerce.
kompat-o, sympathy, pity.
kompren-i, to understand.
kon-i, to know.
konsil-i, to counsel.
konstru-i, to build.
kontraŭ, against.
kred-i, to believe.
kresk-i, to grow.
krom, besides.
krut-a, steep.
kun, with.
kuŝ-i, to lie.
kutim-i, to be accustomed.
kvankam, although.
kvar, four.
kvazaŭ, as if.
kvin, five.

L

la, the.
lac-a, tired.
lag-o, lake.

land-o, land.
lang-o, tongue.
las-i, to let, leave.
laŭ, according to.
leg-i, to read.
legom-o, vegetable.
lern-i, to learn.
lert-a, clever.
lev-i, to raise.
li, he.
lim-o, limit.
lingv-o, language.
lit-o, bed.
long-a, long.
lum-o, light.

M

mal-, prefix denoting the opposite.
malgraŭ, in spite of.
manĝ-i, to eat.
mank-i, to be wanting.
mar-o, sea.
marĉ-o, swamp.
maten-o, morning.
mem, self.
met-i, to put.
mez-o, middle.
mi, I.
mien-o, look, air, gait.
mir-i, to wonder.
mon-o, money.
mond-o, world.
montr-i, to show.
morgaŭ, to-morrow.

Moŝt-o, term of respect: your Highness, Worship, Honour.
mult-a, much, many.

N

-n, ending of accusative; also denotes motion towards and duration of time.
naci-o, nation.
nask-i, to beget.
ne, no, not.
neĝ-o, snow.
neniam, never.
neniu, no one.
ni, we.
nom-o, name.
nov-a, new.
nub-o, cloud.
nun, now.
nur, only.
nutr-i, to feed.

O

-o, ending of nouns.
oft-e, often.
ok, eight.
okazi, to happen.
okul-o, eye.
ol, than.
-on, suffix denoting fraction.
oni, one, people (indef. pron.).
-ont, future participle active.
orel-o, ear.
-os, ending of future.

P

pac-o, peace.
parol-i, to speak.
pen-i, to try.
pens-i, to think.
per, by means of.
perd-i, to lose.
pez-a, heavy.
pied-o, foot.
pint-o, point, peak.
pist-i, to pound.
plaĉ-i, to please.
plat-a, flat.
plej, most.
plen-a, full.
plend-i, to complain.
plenum-i, to fulfil.
pli, more.
plu, more, further, farther.
plug-i, to plough.
popol-o, people, race.
por, for.
pord-o, door.
post, after, behind (time and place).
pov-i, to be able.
pra, original, great-(grandfather).
prav-a, right.
pren-i, to take.
preskaŭ, almost.
pret-a, ready.
preter, beyond, by.
pri, about, concerning.
pro, on account of.

R

rakont-i, to narrate.
ramp-i, to crawl, climb.
rapid-a, quick.
rekt-a, straight.
rem-i, to row.
renkont-i, to meet.
renvers-i, to upset, overthrow.
rikolt-o, crop.

S

sat-a, satisfied, full, replete.
sci-i, to know.
sed, but.
sek-a, dry.
sekv-i, to follow.
sem-o, seed.
sen, without.
sent-i, to feel.
si, self, reflexive pronoun.
sid-i, to sit.
sinjor-o, sir, Mr., gentleman.
skrib-i, to write.
sol-a, alone, only.
son-o, sound.
sonĝ-o, dream.
sonor-a, sonorous.
spec-o, kind, sort.
spert-o, experience.
spir-i, to breathe.
star-i, to stand.
sterk-o, manure.
subit-a, sudden.
sufiĉ-a, sufficient.

supr-a, upper, superior.
sven-i, to swoon.

Ŝ

ŝajn-i, to seem.
ŝerc-i, to joke.
ŝip-o, ship.
ŝirm-i, to shelter.
ŝpar-i, to save up, economize.
ŝtel-i, to steal.

T

tag-o, day.
tamen, yet, nevertheless.
tegment-o, roof.
temp-o, time.
ten-i, to hold, keep.
ter-o, earth.
tial, therefore.
tiel, thus, so.
tiom, so much, so many.
tiu, that.
tra, through.
traf-i, to hit the mark.
trans, across.
tre, very.
trem-i, to tremble.
tro, too much.
tromp-i, to deceive.
trov-i, to find.
trud-i, to shove, thrust.
tuj, immediately.
tut-a, all.

U

-u, ending of imperative-subjunctive.
-uj, suffix denoting "holder."
-ul, suffix denoting characteristic.
unu, one.

V

vapor-o, steam.
vek-i, to wake (trans.)
vel-o, sail.
velk-a, faded.
ven-i, to come.
venk-i, to conquer.
vent-o, wind.
ver-a, true.
vesper-o, evening.
vetur-i, to travel by vehicle (train, carriage, boat, etc.).
vi, you.
vid-i, to see.
vidv-(in)-o, widow(er).
vir-(in)-o, man(woman).
viv-i, to live.
voj-o, way.
vojaĝ-o, voyage, journey.
vokal-o, vowel.
vol-i, to wish.
vom-i, to vomit, be sick.
vort-o, word.

Z

zorg-o : care.

APPENDIX A

SAMPLE PROBLEMS IN REGULAR LANGUAGE

WORD-BUILDING can be made quite an amusing game for children. For instance, give them the suffixes -*ej* (denoting place) and -*il* (denoting instrument), and set them to form words for "school," "church," "factory," "knife," "warming-pan," etc. (*lernejo, preĝejo, fabrikejo, tranĉilo, varmigilo*).

But since the language is perfectly regular in form and construction, and the learner can therefore argue from case to case, it is a useful instrument for instilling clear ideas of grammatical categories. Thus give the roots—

viv-i = to live	*san-a* = healthy	*hom-o* = man
long-a = long	*saĝ-a* = wise	*Di-o* = God
	don-i = to give	

and set such sentences as the following to be worked out—

"He lives long"; "A long life is a gift of God"; "It is wise to live healthily"; "God is divine, man is human"; "Human life is short," etc.

The same roots constantly recur with an -*o*, -*a*, or -*e* tacked on; and the practice in sorting out the endings, and attaching them like labels to nouns, adjectives, verbs, and adverbs, soon marks off the corresponding ideas clearly in the learner's mind.

Analogous to simple sums and conducive to clear thinking are such sentences as the following, for rather more advanced pupils:

Given—

raz-i = to shave	*serv-i* = to serve	*san-a* = healthy
akr-a = sharp	*mort-i* = to die	*ven-i* = to come
uz-i = to use	*hak-i* = to hew	*kun* = with
	sent-i = to feel	

and the table of affixes (pp. 191–2).

Translate—" Constant use had blunted his razor"; " He had his servant shaved " ; " He killed his companion with an axe " ; " Let us send for the doctor."

More advanced exercise (on the same roots) :

Translate—" O Death, where is thy sting ? " " Community of service brings together men subject to death, and dulls the perception of their common mortality.   Willing service dissipates the weariness of the server ; the deadliness of disease is mitigated, and the place of sickness becomes a place of health."

By referring to the table of affixes, the use of which has of course been explained, the learner can work out the answers as follows :

Uz-ad-o estis mal-akr-ig-int-a lian raz-il-on.

Li raz-ig-is sian serv-ant-(*or* ist)on.

Li mort-ig-is sian kun-ul-on per hak-il-o.

Ni ven-ig-u la san-ig-ist-on.

More advanced :

Ho Morto, kie estas via akr-ec-o ?

Kun-servo (*or* kuneco de servo) kun-ig-as la mort-em-(ul)-ojn, kaj mal-akr-ig-as la sent-on de ilia kun-a mort-em-ec-o.   Serv-em-ec-o dis-ig-as la el-uz-it-ec-on de la serv-ant-o ; la mort-ig-ec-o de la mal-san-ec-o mal-akr-iĝ-as, kaj la mal-san-ej-o iĝas san-ej-o.

No national language could be used in this way for building sentences according to rules, and such exercises should give a practical grip of clear use of language.   The student is obliged to analyse the exact meaning of every word of the English sentence, and this necessity inculcates a nice discrimination in the use of words.   At the same time the necessary word-building depends upon clear-headed and logical application of rule. There is no memory work, but the mind is kept on the stretch, and the exercise is wholesome as combating confusion of thought and slovenliness of expression.

APPENDIX B

ESPERANTO HYMN BY DR. ZAMENHOF

La Espero

En la mondon venis nova sento,
Tra la mondo iras forta voko;
Per flugiloj de facila vento
Nun de loko flugu ĝi al loko.
  Ne al glavo sangon soifanta
  Ĝi la homan tiras familion:
  Al la mond' eterne militanta
  Ĝi promesas sanktan harmonion.
Sub la sankta signo de l'espero
Kolektiĝas pacaj batalantoj,
Kaj rapide kreskas la afero
Per laboro de la esperantoj.
  Forte staras muroj de miljaroj
  Inter la popoloj dividitaj;
  Sed dissaltos la obstinaj baroj,
  Per la sankta amo disbatitaj.
Sur neŭtrala lingva fundamento,
Komprenante unu la alian,
La popoloj faros en konsento
Unu grandan rondon familian.
  Nia diligenta kolegaro
  En laboro paca ne laciĝos,
  Ĝis la bela sonĝo de l'homaro
  Por eterna ben' efektiviĝos.

LITERAL TRANSLATION

Hope

Into the world has come a new feeling,
Through the world goes a mighty call;
On light wind-wings
Now may it fly from place to place.
   Not to the sword thirsting for blood
   Does it draw the human family:
   To the world eternally at war
   It promises holy harmony.
Beneath the holy banner of hope
Throng the soldiers of peace,
And swiftly spreads the Cause
Through the labour of the hopeful.
   Strong stand the walls of a thousand years
   Between the sundered peoples;
   But the stubborn bars shall leap apart,
   Battered to pieces by holy love.
On the fair foundation of common speech,
Understanding one another,
The peoples in concord shall make up
One great family circle.
   Our busy band of comrades
   Shall never weary in the work of peace,
   Till humanity's grand dream
   Shall become the truth of eternal blessing.

APPENDIX C

THE LETTER C IN ESPERANTO

$c = ts$ in English "bits."

This has given rise to much criticism. The same sound is also expressed by the letters *ts*. Why depart from the Esperanto principle, " one sound, one letter," and have two symbols (*c* and *ts*) for the same sound ?

A standing difficulty of an international language is : What equivalent shall be adopted for the *c* of national languages ? The difficulty arises owing to the diversity of value and history of the *c* in diverse tongues. Philologists, who know the history of the Latin hard *c* and its various descendants in modern languages, will appreciate this.

(1) Shall *c* be adopted in the international language, or omitted ? If it is omitted, many useful words, which it is desirable to adopt and which are ordinarily spelt with a *c*, will have to be arbitrarily deformed, and this deformation may amount to actual obscuring of their sense. E.g. *cento* = hundred ; *centro* = centre ; *cerbo* = brain ; *certa* = certain ; *cirkonstanco* ▬ circumstance ; *civila* = civil, etc. Such words would become almost unrecognizable for many in the forms *kento, sento, zento, tsento*, etc.

(2) If, then, *c* is retained, what value is to be given to it ? The hard and soft sounds of the English *c* (as in English " cat," " civil ") are already represented by *k* and *s*. Neither of these letters can be dispensed with in the international language ; and it is undesirable to confuse orthographically or phonetically *c*-roots with *s*- or *k*-roots. Therefore another value must be found for the symbol *c*. The choice is practically narrowed down to the Italian soft *c* = *ch*, as in English " church," and the German * *c* = *ts* in English " bits." Now *ch* is a useful and distinctive sound, and has been adopted in Esperanto with a symbol of its own : ĉ. Therefore *ts* remains.

* Also late Latin and early Norman French.

(3) Why not then abolish *c* and write *ts* instead ? For answer, see No. (1) above. It is a worse evil to introduce such monstrosities as *tsento, tsivila,* etc., than to allow two symbols for the same sound, *ts* and *c.* International language has to appeal to the eye as well as to the ear.

This matter of the *c* is only one more instance of the wisdom of Dr. Zamenhof in refusing to make a fetish of slavish adherence to rule. Practical common-sense is a safer guide than theory in attaining the desired goal—ease (of eye, ear, tongue, and pen) for greatest number. In practice no confusion arises between *c* and *ts.*